Outline Studies in
ROMANS

D1520419

Pilkington & Sons
Toll Free 1-888-316-8608
www.pilkingtonandsons.com

Robert Lee Outline Studies Series

Outline Studies in JOHN

Outline Studies in ACTS

Outline Studies in ROMANS

Outline Studies in GALATIANS

Outline Studies in
ROMANS

ROBERT LEE

K

KREGEL PUBLICATIONS
Grand Rapids, Michigan 49501

Library of Congress Cataloging-in-Publication Data

Lee, Robert, 1872-1956.
  Outline Studies in Romans.

  Reprint. Originally published: The Outlined Romans.
London: Pickering & Inglis, [19--].
  1. Bible. N.T. Romans—Sermons—Outlines, syllabi, etc.
I. Title.
BS2665.L39 1987   251'.02   87-3094
ISBN 0-8254-3142-5

1 2 3 4 5 Printing/Year 91 90 89 88 87

Printed in the United States of America

CONTENTS

SECTION 1   DOCTRINAL

ROMANS 1:1—8:39

6 Contents

SECTION 2   DISPENSATIONAL

ROMANS 9:1—11:25

SECTION 3   PRACTICAL

ROMANS 12:1—16:27

Contents 7

PUBLISHER'S PREFACE

Personal and group Bible studies are becoming very popular. It is encouraging to know that Christians — and non-Christians — are taking seriously the study of God's Word. And a good way to get a better understanding of the Bible is to study it book by book!

The *Robert Lee Outline Studies Series* is an excellent study guide to help you discover various books of the Bible. They will help you obtain a better knowledge of God's Word and give you direction in applying it to your life. The expositional outlines, practical notes and illustrations give insights into each passage studied. Preachers and teachers will also find these outlines helpful in their sermon and lesson preparation.

The abbreviations used refer to the following translations: A.V. = Authorized or King James Version; C. & H. = Conybeare and Howson; J. N. D. = Darby's New Testament; M. = Moffatt's translation; R. = *Rotherham's Emphasized Bible*; R.V. = Revised Version; 20 C. = *Twentieth Century New Testament*; W. = Weymouth's *New Testament in Modern Speech*; and Y. = Young's translation.

SECTION 1

DOCTRINAL

ROMANS 1—8

PAUL'S CLEAR TESTIMONY

I. CONCERNING HIMSELF

1. Bond Slave, Called, Set Apart .. .. verse 1
2. Received Grace for Service .. .. .. ,, 5

II. CONCERNING THE GOSPEL

1. God for its **Source** .. .. ,, 1
2. Christ as its **Theme** .. .. ,, 3
3. Son as its **Channel** .. .. ,, 3
4. Christ as its **Glory** .. .. ,, 16
5. Agrees with the Old Testament .. .. ,, 2

III. CONCERNING HIS LORD

1. Of Royal Line .. .. ,, 3
2. **Made** Man .. .. ,, 3
3. Not **made** Son, but declared to be the Son ,, 4
4. His resurrection a proof of His **Divine Sonship**, being God's solemn Amen to the tremendous claims which Christ had made .. .. ,, 4

Proper Credentials. Paul commences his epistle by a reference to himself. This introduction of himself is unusually full, for " it was essential that he should present proper credentials, as he was not known to the Roman Christians."

Purchased Possession. He regarded himself as a slave (see R.V.) of Jesus Christ—the Lord's purchased possession.

Called to the Work. He did not take it up on his own initiative.

Set Apart. He was " set apart " to proclaim the Gospel (see " W ").

The Good News. He calls the Good News :

The Gospel of God—(verse 1) indicating its *source.*
The Gospel of His Son—(verse 9) indicating its *channel.*
The Gospel of Christ—indicating its *message* concerning the Son as the Glorified One.

The Royal Seed. His testimony concerning the Lord Jesus proves that he was perfectly satisfied that Jesus was the Royal Seed.

God Made Son. Jesus did not become Son at His baptism, for at His birth the angels said, " Which is Christ the Lord " (Luke 2. 11). In Isaiah 9, the " child is BORN," but the " *son* is GIVEN."

Obedience. It is a remarkable fact that this Epistle of Faith begins (1. 5) and ends (16. 26) with obedience.

Separated. For " separated " (verse 1) " W " gives " set apart to proclaim."

Declared. For " declared " (verse 4) " C. & H." renders " marked out," and " W." gives " decisively proved."

THE CALLED OF CHRIST

The Lord's people are, as Paul stated the Roman Christians
were, the Lord's

I. CALLED ONES   verse

1. **Our Patron**—the One who calls—" called of "
   or "by Jesus Christ "..   ..   ..   ..   6 A.V.

2. **Our Designation**
   What we are called $\begin{cases} \text{" Called . . . Christ's "} & \text{6 R.V.} \\ \text{" called . . . Saints "} \text{ ..} & \text{7 A.V.} \end{cases}$

3. **Our Vocation**
   What we ought to be $\begin{cases} \text{" called to be Christ's "} & \text{6 R.V.} \\ \text{" called to be Saints "} & \text{7 A.V.} \end{cases}$

4. **Our Obligation**—what we must be—must be
   what we are called, viz., " Saints."

II. BELOVED ONES

Whilst He **loves** the world, His people are **beloved**
of Him   7

III. ENDOWED ONES

Blending of the Greek and Hebrew salutations   7

IV. FAMOUS ONES

Famous for their faith   8

Called. (1) In a crowded court a little man began pushing. On angry
remonstrances being made he said, " Why, have you not heard ? My
name has been called ! " They then gave way. When we discover
that our name has been called, a crowd is sure to be in the way. Push
on and through ; let nothing hinder your response to His gracious call.

(2) The various renderings associated with the word " called " may seem
puzzling ; yet they are suggestive if taken together

Grace to You and Peace. Here we have the blending of the Greek
and Hebrew salutations. " The Greek invariably greeted his friends
with a word which was almost exactly identical with " grace," while the
Hebrew salutation was invariably " peace." These two sum up the
whole of the Gospel—grace is the procuring cause of salvation, whilst
peace is the effect of the possession of salvation.

Beloved of God. Why not say "beloved of God and called " instead
of the order in verses 6 and 7 ? Ah, only those who are the " called "
are the " beloved " ones. The world is loved, but not beloved of God.
Beloved is only used of those who have made a loving response to the
loving invitation.

THE VISIT TO ROME

Seven Reasons why Paul desired to visit the Saints in Rome

I. CAUSE FOR THANKSGIVING
Their noble faith   ..   ..   verse   8

II. REASON FOR FRANKNESS
Proves his deep personal interest in them ..   ,,   9

III. HIS STERLING SINCERITY
" Whom I serve " sincerely ..   ..   ..   ,,   9

IV. UNCEASING PRAYERS
Paul reached more by his prayers than by
his preaching   ..   ..   ,, 9, 10

V. HIS MANLY AFFECTION
" I long to see you " ..   ..   ,,   11

VI. HIS UNSELFISH PURPOSE
To be a channel of blessing   ..   ..   ,,   11

VII. HIS EXPECTED REWARD   ..   ..   ..   ,,   12

The Prosperity of Others.   Do we thank God, as Paul did (verse 8) for the spiritual prosperity of others ?

" **My God** " (verse 8), is a phrase used in the New Testament only by Paul, with the exception of the Lord (who uttered it twice over on the Cross, Matt. 27. 46, and on the resurrection morn once, John 20. 17), and Thomas, who used it once (John 20. 28).

Personal Interest.   One reason why Paul frankly reveals his feelings (verse 9) was that he might prove his deep personal interest in the Roman Christians, and thus pave the way for their acceptance of his message.

" **Serve with my spirit** " (verse 9) might mean either serving God in *sincerity*, or whole-heartedly—from my inmost soul.

" **I am home-sick for a sight of you**," is Bishop Moule's rendering of " I long to see you " (verse 11)

Impart and Receive.   He was anxious to visit them, not only that he might impart some spiritual blessing to them, but that he also might receive one from them.   In watering others we ourselyes get watered.

Verse 9.   " W." renders thus : " To whom I render priestly and spiritual service by telling the good news about His Son.

PAUL'S EXPLANATIONS

Six things he did not want his brethren to be ignorant of

I. THE THWARTING OF MANY OF HIS PLANS

Showing us the need of knowing not only
what God wants us to do, but **when** .. Rom 1. 13

II. THE GLORIOUS FUTURE OF THE JEWISH NATION

Cast off, but not for ever .. .. Rom. 11. 25

III. THE FAILURE OF THE HIGHLY PRIVILEGED

Possibility of missing God's best and
only getting the second best .. .. 1 Cor. 10. 1

IV. THE GIFTS BESTOWED BY THE HOLY SPIRIT FOR SERVICE

To be prized and used .. .. .. 1 Cor. 12. 1

V. THE HEAVY TROUBLE OF OTHERS

Another's burden will help to balance
your own .. .. 2 Cor. 1. 8

VI. THE BLESSED PRIVILEGE OF THE DEPARTED

Sharing Second Advent glories and
privileges .. .. 1 Thess. 4. 13

Favourite Phrases. Most speakers and writers have favourite phrases they often use. " I would not have you ignorant, brethren," seems to have been one of Paul's favourite expressions for drawing attention to some special and important truth, and we note above six uses of the same.

Paul's Planning. Paul evidently made many plans which came to nothing.

Full Realization. Though redeemed, Israel came short of realizing to the full God's purpose for them. See to it that you have God's best for you, and not His second best.

PAUL, THE DEBTOR

I. THE FACT

1. Note the two " I am's "
2. Paul was anxious to visit Rome in order to discharge a debt.
3. Is that the reason why we desire to preach the Gospel ?

II. THE DEBT

1. **Creditor**—All humanity.
2. **Peculiarity**—Debt due for what Another has done.
3. **Nature**—Debt of a Trustee ; Debt of an Ambassador ; Debt of a Brother.
4. **Fruits**—Abolishes all liberty of choice, all thought of virtue, all expectation of praise.

III. THE PAYMENT

1. By preaching a Gospel fitted for all, " to wise and unwise."
2. The only limit to the obligation being, " as much as in me is."

Accountability to God and Man. Daniel Webster, the American States-man, was once asked in a company of friends what thoughts had been the most influential for good on his life and character. After a little pause he said with much feeling : " The thought of my accountability to God." Verily, this is a sobering thought. But Romans 1. 14 and 15, suggests another thought that ought to influence our lives, viz., the thought of our accountability to man.

One Motive Force to Serve. We have already noted several reasons why Paul desired to visit Rome (Study 3). Here is another : He was anxious to visit and labour at Rome *in order to discharge a debt.*

Trustees' Debt. If some one is entrusted with £10 for you, the moment they take possession of that sum they become your debtor. God had entrusted the Gospel to Paul for a perishing world.

Ambassador's Debt. An ambassador entrusted with an important message to a foreign State, is in debt to that State until he has delivered that message. We are the ambassadors of Christ, entrusted by Him with an important message to a perishing world.

Fruits. The consciousness of my indebtedness abolishes—

All thought of liberty of choice. A debtor is not at liberty to choose whether he should pay the debt.

All thought of virtue and expectation of praise. For the debtor is only doing his duty in paying the debt.

THE GOSPEL OF CHRIST

Paul's conception and attestation of its nature and power

I   **ITS   DEFINITION**—" God's spell," *i.e.,* God's   verse
story. Good **news**, not good **advice** ..   ..

II. **ITS SOURCE**—God, not man. God is its author   1. 1

III. **ITS ESSENCE**—Jesus and Him crucified, thus
not a theory, but a Person 1. 3, 16

IV. **ITS NATURE**—A dynamic (power), a mighty,
moving, and propelling force. ..   ..   ..

V. **ITS PURPOSE**—Salvation from
A state of **Condemnation**   ..   ..   ..
A state of **Slavery**   ..   ..
And presently, a state of **Mortality**   ..   ..

VI. **ITS CHANNEL**—" Son " 1. 9

VII. **ITS SCOPE**—Every one. Jew and Gentile   ..

VIII. **ITS   RECEPTION**—Faith.   " Every one that
believeth "   ..   ..

IX. **ITS REVELATION**
Righteousness   17
Love   ..   ..   John 3. 16
Wrath   18

X. **ITS FRUIT**—Life of faith   17
Reveals and **provides** righteousness and grace

Its Name. Gospel is " God's spell." " Spell " is Saxon for story.
Its Essence. A Person, not a theory ; and not a statement merely of the
life of that Person, but the work of that Person ; and the chief work of
that Person was dying.
Its Nature. A dynamic. " Power " is one of Paul's favourite words.
The discoverer of a new and mighty explosive, for a name took the Greek
(rendered power here) and Englishised it, and thus we have dynamite.

R. L. Stevenson, in his " Travels with a Donkey," writes : " I met but
one human being that forenoon, a dark, military-looking wayfarer, who
carried a game-bag on a baldrick but he made a remark which seems
worthy of record. For when I asked him if he were a Protestant or Catholic,
" Oh," said he, " I make no shame of my religion. I am a Catholic." Paul
had a religion he was not ashamed of. The reason of his long delay in
visiting Rome was not because he was ashamed of the Gospel, though
Rome was the centre of the world's wisdom.

THE RIGHTEOUSNESS OF GOD

I. ITS DEFINITION in the light of this Epistle : "That consistency with His own revealed character whereby God receives sinful man on the ground of the work of Christ."

II. IT IS THE PRE-EMINENT THEME in this Epistle: Righteousness, not love, is the primary theme of Romans.

III. ITS CONTINUOUS UNVEILING in the Gospel : The glory of the Gospel is that it **has** unveiled, and **keeps** unveiling to every seeking soul, the Righteousness of God. "Is being revealed." (W).

IV. ITS PROVISION in the Son : God's Righteousness is a Person (Jer. 23. 5, 6).

V. ITS BESTOWAL is conditioned on Faith : Faith, strictly speaking, is Righteousness, being the

1. Supreme act of Righteousness
2. Unites with Christ the Righteous One
3. Blossoms out into a life of Righteousness

Another Way Open. A working man had trouble with his eyes, and consulted his doctor, who said, " There are two cataracts growing over your eyes, and your only hope of preserving your sight is to go and see Dr.——. I would advise you to go at once ; and don't forget to take several pounds in your pocket, for you might find the fee heavy." The working man had £20 in the bank, and drew it out. The Specialist examined his eyes and then said : " I am not sure whether you can pay the fee ? I never take less than a hundred guineas." Then said the working man, " I must go blind, and remain so." The Specialist replied : " You cannot come up to my terms, and I cannot come down to yours, but there is another way open—I can perform the operation gratis." You cannot come up to the requirements of God's Holy Law, neither can God abate His claims, and come down to the level of our plan in accepting anything that man may think sufficient. But He can and does act on another ground, that of grace. This Epistle shows that grace reigns through and in, righteousness.

" **Hold the truth in unrighteousness** ' (verse 18). It is possible to know the truth, and yet remain ungodly.

THE REVELATION OF GOD

I. A KNOWLEDGE OF GOD

1. **This is possible apart from revelation.** " That which may be known of God," or that which is knowable of God   ..   ..   verse 19

2. **This can be acquired apart from revelation,** because of our reasoning powers. " For God hath shewed it "   ..   ..   ..   „   19

II. A WITNESS TO GOD

1. **There is a witness within us**—conscience— to the existence of the Divine Being. " Is manifest in them "   ..   ..   ..   „   19

2. **There is a witness without us**—in nature, history, and man's being—to the power, personality, wisdom, and justice of the Divine Being   ..   ..   „   20

" **That which may be known of God** " (verse 19), implies that there may be many things concerning God which can be known apart from revelation. This proves that there is no valid reason for ignorance of God.

" **His eternal power and Godhead.**" The Power, the Personality, and the Eternity of God.

" **For God hath shewed it.**" That is to say, God has endued us with reason to grasp and comprehend what is to be seen. Man may not be able to see much of God in nature ; yet what is to be seen can be seen clearly if only he will take the trouble to use the powers God has given.

The Light of Nature. Though the heathen world has not the light of revelation, it has the dim light of nature and creation.

" **Is manifest in them.**' This might mean—is clear and plain to the inmost conscience ; or is this not a reference to the intuitive faculty in man which, apart from reasoning or intellectual acquirements, compel us to admit the existence of God. What instinct is to the insect, bird, or animal, this faculty is to man.

THE WRATH OF GOD

Why the Wrath of God is justly over Heathendom

I. THEY DEFLECT THE LIGHT

They do not live up to the light they have .. verse 18

II. THEY NEGLECT THE TESTIMONY

They are criminally neglectful of the testimony
of Creation ..   .. vv. 19, 20

III. THEY REJECT THE TRUTH

They are guilty of deliberate rejection of truth
once held ..   .. vv. 21-32

A Paralysing Change. A great change has come over the professing Church's conception of the peril of the heathen world, as will be seen by the following statement : " Now the motive behind modern missionary enterprise is not to rescue a heathen world from the wrath of God and everlasting punishment, but to enlighten them, and lead them to share with us the glorious blessings and privileges of the Christian faith here and now, for present and temporal advantage." All this sounds learned and charitable, but it is both unscriptural and paralysing to Christian effort.

Scripture Declaration. The Scripture here declares that the wrath of God overhangs the whole heathen world (verse 18). " But," say some, " that is most unreasonable—fancy condemning and punishing people for something they do not know ! " The Outline above answers that question.

" **They hold the truth.**" They have a knowledge of Divine things ; but they hold it " in unrighteousness," *i.e.*, they do not live up to that truth.

" **They are neglectful.**" This is an important argument from the standpoint of natural religion (see Study No. 8).

" **They are backsliders.**" Instead of a man by his own unaided efforts emerging into a clear and pure conception of God, the contrary is the actual fact. Verses 21 to 32 clearly prove that all nations are backsliders from pure truth once possessed, proving the *descent* not the *ascent* of man.

Guilty of Rejection of Truth. This is important. Here is declared the fact that the heathen world is guilty of wilful rejection of truth, whether revealed to them, or discovered by processes of human reasoning. How important these days to know precisely the actual teaching of the Word of God !

MORAL RUIN UNIVERSAL

I. INITIAL STEPS IN THE DOWNWARD TRACK

1. Did not yield the adoration, or
2. The gratitude due to Him   ..   ..   verse 21

II. RESULTS OF GETTING AWAY FROM GOD

1. False Philosophy   ..   ..   ..   verse 21
2. Warped Affections   ..   ..   ..   ,, 21
3. Foolish Wisdom   ..   ..   ..   ,, 22
4. Idolatry ..   ..   ,, 23

III. RELEASE OF THE DIVINE RESTRAINT

The awful results consequent on this are seen
in three successive stages marked by
phrase, " God ... gave up "   ..   vv. 24, 26, 28

The Dignity of Man. We generally trace the dignity of man by noting his intuitions, his capacities for worship, and his longings. But we may also see his greatness by his awful ruin and total depravity. ' It is just in this way we form our conceptions of ancient dynasties, and the magnificence of ancient works and cities. We reason like this. If the ruins are so magnificent, how glorious must that city or monument have been in its unfallen state ! So is it with man. Our saddest impressions of his original greatness is to be derived from the magnificent ruin he displays. The picture drawn of man in this chapter is not that of a feeble and effeminate creature, but of one vile, terrible, swift, destructive, fierce, fearless, great in evil, and miserable in greatness."

" **God gave them up** " does not mean that God exerted any positive influence in inducing them to sin, but simply that He ceased to restrain them.

" **Inventors of evil things.**" This is in 20 C. as " They invented new sins."

" **Which are not convenient** " is rendered by C. & H. " that are unseemly."

Paul's Underlying Purpose. It is important to note Paul's underlying purpose, viz., to trace the universality of sin, the justness of the wrath of God, and the universal need of the Gospel.

SELF-RIGHTEOUS JUDGES

The enlightened Gentile and the highly privileged Jew alike
condemned

I. THE ENLIGHTENED GENTILE, living in the feeble light of natural religion

1. Practised the very thing he condemned in others   .. ..   verse 1

2. Consequently was without excuse ..   .. ,, 1

3. The absolute impartiality of the justice and judgment of God ..   ..   ,, 2

4. And the impossibility of escape from that judgment ..   ..   ,, 3

II. THE HIGHLY PRIVILEGED JEW, living in the possession of the clear light of revealed religion

1. Great **Advantage** of the Jew ..   .. .. vv. 17, 18

2. Great **Mission** of the Jew   .. .. .. vv. 19, 20

3. Great **Condemnation** of the Jew   .. .. vv. 21-24

Practice and Profession. A fountain pen agent had spent half an hour with a prosperous merchant commending the use of that article, had secured an order for 500, and was writing the order down in his note book, when the merchant exclaimed, "Hold on, sir, I cancel that order," and turned to wait on a customer. The commercial left the shop in disgust. Later, the merchant's book-keeper said, "Why did you cancel that fountain pen order ?" "Why ?" said the man, "Because he talked fountain pens to me for half an hour, using a number of forcible arguments, *and then booked my order with a lead pencil. His practice did not agree with his profession.*" Macaulay says of Steele, "His life was spent in sinning and repenting ; in inculcating what was right, and doing what was wrong. In speculation he was a man of piety and honour ; in practice he was much of the rake, and a little of the swindler." There are many whose practice does not agree either with their profession or knowledge. That class amongst Gentile and Jew, Paul had in mind in Romans 2 and 3.

MAN'S SUICIDAL FOLLY

On the part of the World in amassing Divine Wrath

I. DESPISING

1. **What?** God's riches (see Rom. 9. 23 ; 11. 33 ; Eph. 1. 7 ; 2. 4, 7).

2. **How?** By thinking lightly of, and treating with neglect.

3. **Why?** Through misunderstanding the purpose of His goodness and grace.

II. TREASURING

1. **What?** Wrath.

2. **Why?** Fruit of a hard and impenitent heart.

3. **For When?** The Day of Wrath.

Suicidal Folly. A friend, whilst travelling on the Canadian Pacific Railway, was able, when the train stopped at a siding in a lonely place, to get off and walk about. Whilst doing so he saw lumps of ore the colour of gold, and thought he had struck a gold mine, until a fellow-traveller proved he was mistaken. What would you have thought if these had been real nuggets of gold, and mixed with them were bars of dynamite, and yet wide awake folk despised the gold and pocketed the dynamite ? This is precisely a parable of what the world is doing. Paul was addressing the intelligent, self-righteous Gentile, and he charged them with this folly.

God's Goodness Mistaken. The supreme revelation of God's goodness in the Cross of Christ, and His goodness shown in the exercise of His gentleness and forbearance towards sinners, was and is designed and adapted to produce repentance, yet His gentleness is mistaken for weakness, forbearance for indifference, and longsuffering for indulgence.

Treasure in Hell. There is such a thing as laying up treasure in Hell as well as in Heaven.

Amassing Wrath. What an awful idea is expressed in verse 5 : " that the sinner himself is amassing, like hoarded treasure, an ever accumulating stock of Divine Wrath, to burst upon him in that dreadful day ! "

FAITH AND WORKS

An examination of some explanations given for Paul's strange
Emphasis on Works in a treatise on Faith

I. **THE EXPLANATION OF ISOLATION,** *i.e.*, that the question of regards and punishments is here isolated from the main subject of the Epistle.

This view is unsatisfactory.

II. **THE EXPLANATION OF LEGALITY**, *i.e.*, that man is viewed apart from grace, seeking eternal life by well doing.

This view is good, but not wholly satisfactory.

III. **THE EXPLANATION OF REWARD,** *i.e.*, that eternal life is viewed not only as a present possession, but as a future reward for devoted life and service.

Truth, yet not the truth here.

IV. **THE EXPLANATION OF THE EPISTLE OF JAMES,** *i.e.*, that the final judgment will turn upon character alone, and a transformed and transfigured character is the fruit and proof of justification by faith.

The true view which is in harmony with the whole Epistle.

"**According to his Works**" (R V.). That sounds strange! I thought man would be dealt with according to his faith and not according to his works? Are we saved by our deeds? Eternal life the reward of holiness—— I thought it is a gift, given and received on the merit of Christ, and not on the ground of works

Works the Fruit of Faith. "Thus, at the very beginning of this letter, the master-theme, of which is salvation by faith, we have an overwhelming and unanswerable indictment of that particular heresy to which an improper emphasis of the doctrine is liable to give rise. Nothing can be clearer than the Apostle's teaching, that works will be the final test of Judgment; faith, which does not produce these, is declared useless. Godliness as privileged relationship is of no value except it produces actual righteousness" (G. Campbell Morgan).

THE JUDGMENT OF GOD

The Gentile World at the Bar of God and Conscience

I. **ABSOLUTELY JUST** .. .. .. verses 2, 5

II. **ABSOLUTELY CERTAIN** .. .. .. ,, 3

III. **ABSOLUTELY UNIVERSAL** .. .. ,, 6

IV. **BASED ON CHARACTER** as revealed by
conduct .. .. ,, 6-9

V. **ABSOLUTELY IMPARTIAL** .. .. ,, 11

VI. **PERFECTLY REASONABLE** .. .. ,, 12-15

VII. **STILL IN THE FUTURE** .. .. .. ,, 16

VIII. **BY THE LORD JESUS CHRIST** .. .. ,, 16

" **Difficult to Grasp.**" Speaking frankly, the verses before us are difficult
to fathom and grasp. This Outline should be a help

" **Saved Without Law.**" This is not a question of salvation, but the
judgment of the heathen. There is nothing in verse 12 about being saved
without law.

" **The Law of Conscience.**" "While there is but one principle of Divine
Judgment for all, yet the standards of judgment will necessarily be different
for Jews and Gentiles. The standard of the Jew will be the Law of Moses;
but the standard of the Gentile will be the law of conscience."

" **The Light of Conscience.**" Some Gentiles do actually some (not all)
things the law of Moses commanded, such as honesty, purity, etc. This
proves that God has not left the heathen world without some light, the
light of conscience and of a moral sense.

Observe, no Gentile can be, or ever has been, found, who has not acted
contrary to the light of their own conscience. The close connection of
verses 15 and 16 suggests that when they stand before the Bar of God they
will also stand before the bar of their own conscience, and will admit the
rightness of God's judgment.

CIRCUMCISION

The Circumcision of the Flesh and the Circumcision of the Spirit

I. ITS ORIGIN   ..   ..   Gen. 17 10-14

II. ITS DESIGN
Sign and Seal, indicating character within   Rom. 4. 11

III. ITS DESECRATION   ..   ..   ..   Rom. 2. 25-27

IV. ITS SUCCESSOR
Gift of Holy Spirit (Eph. 1. 13 ; Gal.
4. 6 ; Col. 2. 11), ...   Rom. 2. 28, 29

An Abrupt Introduction. Observe how abruptly the apostle introduces the subject of circumcision. It would seem that he anticipated the Jews bringing forth this their last and strongest argument.

God its Author. If one reflects for a moment upon the measure of painfulness and mutilation involved in the operation, one can hardly imagine man to be its originator. God was its Author.

A Sign and a Seal. It was *an outward sign of an inward change.* A shop sign is an outward sign of the business done within. As a sign, its primary idea was that of cutting off, *i.e.*, separation from the world to God. It meant that the whole being of the circumcised must be considered as His. *As a Seal* it was God's mark of ownership.

Profession and Practice. The Jews desecrated circumcision by parting asunder what God had joined, viz., profession and practice. They mistook the sign for what it signified.

Real Circumcision. It is quite clear by above Scriptures that Baptism of the Spirit and not of Water has taken the place of circumcision. Real circumcision is that of the heart. That the old circumcision had a real spiritual and moral significance is indicated by the following Scriptures : Circumcised lips (Exod. 6. 12), ears (Jer. 6. 10), heart (Jer. 4. 4 ; Lev. 26. 41 ; Deut. 10. 16 ; Acts 7. 51).

JEW AND GENTILE

A Brief Controversial Dialogue Between Paul and an
Unconverted Jew

I. If your Assertion be true that Jew and Gentile are on the same spiritual level, and stand equally condemned before God, then does it not prove

1. That ordinances are of no value at all ?   .. verse 1
    Paul's reply ..   ..   ,,   2
2. That there is no advantage whatever in
    being a Jew ?   ..   ..   ,,   1
    Paul's reply ..   ..   ,,   2
3. That God has broken His Covenant Pro-
    mises ?   ..   ..   ,,   3
    Paul's reply ..   ..   ,,   4
4. And that only on account of the unfaithful-
    ness of a few ?   ..   ..   ,,   3
    Paul's reply ..   ..   ,,   4

II. If your Assertion that man's faithlessness and sin only bring out into clearer light the faithfulness, righteousness, and glory of God

1. Then God cannot justly punish man for the
    sin which does such good service ? ..   ..   ,,   5
    Paul's reply ..   ..   ,,   6
2. And would it not be advisable for man to
    sin more and more in order to bring still
    greater glory to God ?   ..   ..   ..   ,,   7
    Paul's reply ..   ..   ,,   8

III. You Assert that there is, after all, advantage in being a Jew

If so, then the Jew is superior to the Gentile
in every sense ?   ..   ..   ,,   9
    Paul's reply ..   ..   ,,   9

Paul's Case Proved. The first great section of this Epistle has now really closed. Paul has proved that Jew and Gentile are alike unrighteous, that they are alike under sin, and stand condemned before God. But instead of summing up as he does in 3, 9 to 20, he makes a digression to meet certain objections.

Paul's Wordy Combats. These verses must be synagogue echoes, a controversial dialogue Paul must often have had there, a skeleton of many of his wordy combats.

FALLEN MAN'S PORTRAIT
A True Likeness as Revealed in the Bible

I. CHARACTER

1. Negative.
- None righteous .. .. .. verse 10
- None understandeth .. .. ,, 11
- None seeketh .. .. .. ,, 11

2. Positive.
- Out of the way .. .. .. ,, 12
- Worthless .. .. ,, 12

II. CONDUCT

1. Words.
- Throat .. .. ,, 13
- Tongue .. .. ,, 13
- Lips .. .. ,, 13
- Mouth .. .. ,, 14

2. Actions.
- Feet .. .. vv. 15-17
- Eyes .. .. verse 18

Quotations from Old Testament. The long, clear, convincing argument to prove man's ruin now draws to a close. Paul sums up in the light of the Old Testament, bringing forward quotations from the Septuagint version of Psalms, Proverbs, and Isaiah.

Under Sin. It is interesting to observe the word " sin " (9) for the first time in this Epistle. He has been dwelling upon it without mentioning it. "Under" is a very strong word, implying *bondage as well as guilt.*

A Perfect Mosaic. Here we have God's portrait of fallen man—and these Scriptures form a perfect mosaic, as above outline shows.

Character Before Conduct. Observe that, in harmony with the whole of Scripture, *character is dealt with before conduct, and speech before actions.*

Other Versions. Verse 10, 20 C., renders, " Not one who stands right before God ; " " Gone out of the way," verse 12, R.V., gives, " Turned aside ; " " Become unprofitable," verse 12, Bishop H. Moule renders it, " Have turned worthless." And 20 C. renders verse 16, " Distress and trouble dog their steps."

THE LAW

I. ITS IDENTITY

Or the Apostolic view of the authority of the Old Testament.

II. ITS VITALITY

Its voice loud and clear.

III. ITS AUDIENCE

Only those to whom it was expressly given.

IV. ITS MISSION

1. Originally intended as an **instrument of instruction.**
2. Failing obedience, it becomes the **instrument of conviction,** producing a sense of human impotence.

V. ITS SUCCESS

Every voice of self defence or excuse silenced.

All Mouths Stopped. Before Paul mentions Justification he sees that all mouths are stopped. But the difficulty is how to accomplish this. That is the work of the Law.

Paul's " Dead Certs." " We know," one of Paul's characteristic words. Note eight of Paul's " dead certs : " True Mission of Law (Rom. 3. 18) ; True Nature of Law (Rom. 7. 14) ; Creation (Rom. 8. 22) ; Events of Life (Rom. 8. 28) ; Idols (1 Cor. 8. 1 and 4) ; Heavenly Home (2 Cor. 5. 1) ; The Lord (Heb. 10. 30).

The Old Testament. Paul here means by Law, the Old Testament Scriptures, which he points out as full of vitality. " The Law SAITH."

The Two Laws. Paul has referred to two Laws : (1) The Unwritten Law, the law of conscience (chap. 1. 19), which speaks to those who have not the Written Law. (2) The Written Law, which appeals to all who have it, to the Jew first specially, and also to the Gentile.

Needle and Thread. " I am so glad you use needle and thread,' remarked a minister of the Gospel to his guest, an Evangelist, who had just commenced a Gospel campaign in that town. " Oh yes," was the reply, " as I am away from home so much, I never come away without those commodities." " Ah, but I don't mean that," remarked the minister, " I mean your preaching. You use the law (the needle) which pierces and wounds, before you use the Gospel (the thread) to bind up.'

RIGHTEOUSLY JUSTIFIED

I. JUSTIFICATION DEFINED

1. More than pardon.
2. It is to **declare** or to **pronounce righteous**.
3. Not to **make** righteous, for that is sanctification.

II. GOD JUSTIFIED

1. Prominent thought is God's righteousness in justifying the ungodly who trust in the Lord Jesus.
2. The righteousness of this act declared and explained by the Cross (vv. 25, 26).

III. SINNER JUSTIFIED

God's right method :

1. Manifested	verse 21
2. Witnessed	,, 21
3. Provided	vv. 22, 24
4. Available for all	vv. 22, 23, 29, 30
5. Enjoyed only by faith	vv. 22, 28
6. Granted freely	verse 24
7. In favour	,, 24
8. Excludes boasting	,, 27
9. Establishes the Law	,, 31

Justified Freely. In the biography of Sir Arthur Blackwood, a friend writes : " I recollect his saying another day how he had been living for a week on these two words, ' Justified freely ' " (verse 24).

Justification and Pardon. Sir W. Robertson Nicoll stated that " one of the great errors of modern evangelicalism has been to identify justification with pardon. Justification is more than pardon. To justify means to declare or to pronounce righteous ... We receive justification in the present and unchangeable forgiveness of sins through the blood of the atonement."

Spurgeon's Power. Dr. Dale said with much truth that the great secret of C. H. Spurgeon's power was that he was always fully conscious of his own free justification before God.

The Very Heart. We have here the very heart of this Epistle, a portion well worth our deepest thought.

Righteousness. The word Righteousness is used for : (1) God's Character. (2) God's Action, or (3) God's Gift.

We have the righteousness of the Act of God in verses 25 and 26; and the *gift* of righteousness as seen in justification, in verses 21 to 24, and 27 to 31, a gift bestowed in absolute rightness.

Justifying Yet Just. Philip Mauro says : " It seems clear that the thought to which the Spirit of God gives prominence in this passage is, not the justifying of the unrighteous, but God's righteousness in justifying those who are of the faith of Jesus ; " and what is of the greatest importance in God's sight is, not that the sinner should be justified, but that God in justifying him might Himself be just.

THE DEATH OF CHRIST

Why the Lord Jesus Suffered Death so Conspicuously

I. FACT

1. " Set forth " means to place in public view, to exhibit in a conspicuous situation.

2. Verily this is a fact. Our Lord was made on the Cross a spectacle to men and to angels.

II. NEGATIVE

His death, but not His conspicuous death, was necessary to make atonement and propitiation.

III. POSITIVE

1. He suffered conspicuously to openly and triumphantly justify the forbearance of God toward the penitent **who lived from the time of Adam to Christ** (v. 25).

2. And to openly and triumphantly **justify the present act of God** in justifying the unrighteous who believe in Jesus (v. 26).

Cowper's Conversion. Verse 25 will ever be memorable as the means of the conversion of Cowper the poet, at St. Albans, in 1764.

Redemption and Propitiation. Here are two aspects of the death of Christ—His death is viewed as a redemption, and as a propitiation. The latter deals more particularly with the guilt of sin, and the former with the bondage of sin.

God's Past Forbearance. Here is a difficulty : While God had proclaimed His Law, and had not yet proclaimed His Gospel, yet He did bear with sinners ; did He think lightly of sin ? No. Verse 25 is the answer. *God's past forbearance was exercised in virtue of what Jesus was to do in the fulness of time on the Cross.*

God's Present Forbearance. That solves the past; but what about the present ? Verse 26 deals with that.

Wonderfully Satisfied Holiness. " Christ's sacrifice does not persuade God to have mercy, for He is Eternal Love already, but liberates His love along the line of a wonderfully satisfied holiness."

JUSTIFICATION BY FAITH

Paul declares Justification by Faith to be no New Doctrine

I. DAVID

1. **Described** it as a blessed state .. .. verse 6
2. **Defined** it as a state of
   (a) Forgiveness of sin by God
   (b) Forgetfulness of sin by God
   (c) Deliverance from guilt .. .. vv. 7, 8

II. ABRAHAM

1. Possessed and enjoyed this blessedness .. vv. 3, 9
2. Through faith .. .. vv. 3, 5, 22
3. Long before he was circumcised .. .. verse 10
4. Circumcision did not **confer,** but **confirmed**
   that righteousness .. .. „ 11
5. The Abrahamic covenant, too, was of grace .. „ 13

Nothing New. Often do we find ourselves repeating the utterance of the Preacher that " there is no new thing under the sun " (Eccles. 1. 9).

Not a Pauline Doctrine. That is so with Justification by Faith. Paul's teaching concerning Justification seemed new and revolutionary to the people of his day ; but he affirmed that this great doctrine was not only foreshadowed but actually enjoyed ages before his time. Is it not therefore wrong to call it a Pauline doctrine ?

Its Possession. Observe, before we read of its blessedness, we read of its possession. I must possess it before I can enjoy, and thoroughly define it.

A Blessed State. Justification by Faith David describes as a "blessed," not a happy state. It is possible for us to actually be in this blessed state and not be happy. It is when our justified state is realised by us that we then exult in God.

Works and Faith. Salvation by Works brings glory to man (verse 2). Salvation by Faith brings glory to God.

R.V. Change. Observe the change the R.V. makes in verse 19.

CHRIST'S RESURRECTION

What our Lord's Resurrection had to do with our Justification

I. NEGATIVE

1. There is no atoning merit or value in it.
2. It is the blood that maketh atonement.

II. POSITIVE

1. **It was God's Signature** to (indicating full settlement of) the account that stood against us. (Note Matt. 5. 26).

2. **It was the Divine Proclamation** of our justification in the Person of our Substitute.

8. **It is God's Pledge** that resurrection, which is ours positionally, will ultimately be ours experimentally and literally as well as spiritually.

4. **It provides THE Test of Real Faith** (faith, not merely on God, but on the God of the Resurrection).

5. **It provides us with the Object of Faith,** an ever-living Saviour.

Delivered. This is a very strong word. It means that He was deliberately handed over to death. The great attraction of the Gospel is its story of redeeming love. It is said that the Moravian missionaries to Greenland toiled for years teaching the natives about the Creation, the Fall, Flood, etc., all to no purpose. But one day John Beck read to a small company of them the sad story of Christ's redeeming and dying love. One of them, Kayamak by name, with tears streaming down his face, said to him, " Tell me once more, for I, too, would be saved." At last the missionaries had found the key to the Greenlanders' hearts.

The Account Against Us. If you saw one who had been imprisoned for debt at liberty, with Matthew 5. 26 in mind, you would conclude that the debt had been fully met. Christ's release from the prison-house of death is a proof of the completeness of His atonement, and that what He has done for us was accepted. His resurrection tells us that God is FOR us.

Divine Proclamation of our Justification. This is a deeper thought. Our sin had killed Him ; our justification raised Him again. It is not merely the pledge of our resurrection ; it is our resurrection in Him.

The Test of Faith. " Oh, I believe God," many say. " But what about God do you believe ? " we would reply. It is important to note that it is *the God of the Resurrection* we are to believe in. See verses 17 and 24 ; also Romans 10. 9.

JUSTIFICATION BLESSINGS

I. PAST

1. Note force of " Therefore."
2. As to guilt we are justified.
3. And the old enmity and hostility between God and man, and man and God, gone.

II. PRESENT

1. **Peace** :   (a)   of conscience, through the *mercy* of God.
             (b)   of heart, through the *love* of God.
             (c)   of mind, through the *truth* of God.
             (d)   of soul, through the *presence* of God

2. **Access** :   (a)   Into favour with God.
             (b)   Into communion with God.

3. **New Standing** :
             (a)   From condemnation.
             (b)   From slipping.

4. **New View of Trouble** :
             (a)   Through certainty concerning future.
             (b)   Through recognising effects on character.

III. FUTURE

" We exult in hope of some day sharing His glory " (W.).

The Shining Face. In the convent library at Erfurt is a picture of Luther, the young monk of four-and-twenty. He is gazing into the open pages of a huge Latin Bible. We see it is the early chapters of Romans. A bit of broken chain indicates that the Bible was once chained, but it is now free, and his own. The sweet light of morning, shining in at the open lattice, is reflected from the page upon his keen, anxious face. An emblem of the light of Heaven, shining in his soul through the great truth declared in Romans 5. 1. Our faces are bound to shine when we possess and enjoy this great religious experience.

The Fruits. The firstfruit of justification is *peace* ; the second is full and blessed *access* ; the third is a safe and sure *standing* ; and the fourth an altogether *new view of sorrow*.

MENTION OF THE SPIRIT

The First Time the Holy Spirit is Mentioned in this Epistle

I. ITS SIGNIFICANCE

1. What to Think

Christ's work *for* me should engage my thoughts before the Spirit's work within me.

2. What to Preach

Christ's work *for* us, and not the work of the Spirit, should be the subject of my preaching to dead souls.

II. ITS TEACHING

The Bestowal of the Holy Spirit—

1. Is the pledge of the ultimate **full realisation of all our hopes**.

2. Gives to mind and heart a **vivid realisation of the love of God.**

3. Pours into heart and life like a torrent, **the very love of God.**

First Reference to Spirit. That this is the first reference to the Holy Spirit in this wonderful Epistle is full of teaching.

Preaching to Dead Souls. Someone had been taking Sir Arthur Blackwood to task for not preaching about the Holy Spirit. In a reply dated, May, 1861, he writes : " Believe me, I do desire to honour mightily the Blessed Spirit, and cease not to implore that He will accompany the Word, and convince as only He can and must. I have no confidence in anything else, but I cannot see the rightness of preaching the work of the Holy Ghost to dead souls, instead of the work of that Jesus of whom He testifies."

Proof of Bestowal. The proof of the bestowal of the Holy Spirit is the love of God within.

DIVINE LOVE PROVED

Love for the Powerless and Loveless Commended and Proved,
but not Created, by the Cross

I. HUMAN LOVE

1. Would not lead to self-sacrifice for the merely
   just and upright man .. .. .. verse 7
2. Though it might do so for a lovable man .. „ 7

II. DIVINE LOVE

Has sacrificed for

1. The criminally powerless man (weak through
   sin) .. .. „ 6
2. The impious and irreverent man (ungodly
   means, for one thing, irreverent) .. „ 6
3. The man who comes short .. .. .. „ 8
   (A sinner is one who comes short)
4. The man in enmity .. .. „ 10
   The above four points give a fourfold picture
   of our state by nature.

The Missing Note. Have you missed anything in this Epistle up to
now ? Have you not missed the love note ? Though the Apostle has
carefully proved the ruin of man and the righteousness of God, he has not
made any reference so far concerning the love of God.

God's Love Proved. Having now mentioned God's love, he shows the
amazing character of that love by a series of contrasts between the love of
God and the love of man. He shows that where human love ends Divine
love commences. *Thus God's love is not only commended but proved.*

Weymouth's Renderings. There are some strikingly beautiful renderings
in Weymouth's version which the reader ought to consult.

Useful and Attractive. Observe the merely good and upright man
may be a trifle hard because rigidly just, therefore not likely to move a
heart to sacrifice on his account. M'Cheyne, commenting on Song of
Solomon 4. 6, said : " Some believers were a garden that had fruit trees,
and so were *useful*, but we ought to have spices, and be *attractive*."

We ought to be good and lovable, hence attractive. " Be a good man,
Lockhart, be a good man," said Sir Walter Scott, to his son-in-law, as
he lay dying.

SAVED BY CHRIST'S LIFE

THOSE SAVED BY HIS DEATH He Keeps Saved by His Risen and Glorified Life

I. AS A PATIENT IS SAVED
by the Life of his Doctor.

II. AS A CHILD IS SAVED
by the Life of the Mother.

III. AS AN OFFICIAL IS SAVED WHEN ABSENT
by the life of a Friend at Court.

IV. AS AN ARMY IS SAVED
by the Life of its General.

Life or Death ? " Saved by His life ? " What is the meaning of this ? " I always thought we were saved by His death ! "

A Message to the Reconciled. You will observe that this is a message to reconciled ones, to those who have already been saved by the atoning death. " Being NOW justified " (verse 9), " *being* reconciled " (verse 10).

Which Life. " Saved by His life." Which life ? Let it be clearly understood that Paul is not referring to *the life of our Lord lived before the Cross.* Studying that life shames, not saves. Neither is he referring to the *life poured out for us at Calvary,* nor to *the life given to us* by the indwelling Spirit, though of course both these save. He is referring to Christ's risen and glorified life on high—priestly service, lived for us in the presence of God.

The Family Doctor. As a patient is saved by the life of his doctor. " If only the old family doctor had been alive, he would have pulled him through, for he understood the case perfectly," is sometimes heard. Jesus ever lives, therefore can save to the uttermost.

Mother's Attention. " If only mother had been alive, and could have looked well after the child, then it would, humanly speaking, have lived," we have heard remarked.

A Friend at Court. In Eastern Countries, enemies plot the disgrace and ruin of an absent official. Happy is he if he has a friend at Court to protect his interests. We have, in the Lord Jesus, a Friend at Court to defend us from the attacks of our adversary

Our Captain Immortal. Many an army has been annihilated when the General fell. Our Captain is immortal. He ever lives.

THE FOUR MONARCH'S

I. WHAT UNION WITH ADAM HAS MEANT FOR US

1. **Sin** as a Monarch has reigned   .. vv. 21, 12-14
2. **Death** as a Monarch reigned ..   ..   .. vv. 14, 21
   " Death became king " (Bishop Moule's rendering).

II. WHAT UNION WITH CHRIST SHOULD MEAN TO US

1. **Grace** as a Monarch might reign   .. vv. 21, 15-20
2. **Believers** may as Monarchs reign in life   .. verse 17

The Construction of this Portion

1. Statement   ..   .. verse 12
2. Argument   ..   .. vv. 13, 14
3. Comparison   ..   .. vv. 15-21

The Logical Centre. This section before us is an argument profound and weighty, and it has occasioned an immense deal of critical and theological discussion.   Yet, it is a section of great value in the study of this Epistle, for " these verses give us the logical centre of the Epistle," in fact " gives organic life " to the entire letter.

Solidarity. This is a word much to the front in these days.   The solidarity of the human race is a modern doctrine held by all thinking men. " Here we have a spiritual and theological illustration of this great modern principle of solidarity."   The Bible declares there is a solidarity for evil and a solidarity for good.   Man's connection with Adam involved him in sin and death—when he fell, all the human family fell in him (as for illustration, when a Prime Minister falls he drags his party with him).   But there is a new and gracious solidarity—man's connection with Christ through personal and living faith means glory both now and ever after.

Much More. This phrase occurs in verses 9, 10, 15, 17, and 20, and is the message of verses 15 to 21.   What we have derived from Adam we derive " much more " from Christ ; " we gain infinitely more in Christ than we ever lost in Adam.

Original Sin. The doctrine of " original sin " is denounced by many, but solidarity includes it, and gives a modern presentation of it.

JUSTIFICATION AND SIN

I. A QUESTION
Does not justification by grace encourage sin ?   verse   1

II. A PROTEST
A reply repelling this thought with scorn   ..   ,,   1

III. A STATEMENT
We died to sin (see R.V.), we died in Him   ..   ,,   2

IV. AN EXPLANATION
Baptism means burial and resurrection   ..   vv. 3-5

V. AN APPLICATION
" Knowing this,"—do we know it ? ..   .. verse   6

Compromise with Sin. It was said of Mark Pattison that " he spent all his life in the tents of compromise." What a wretched life to lead ! Robertson Nicoll has finely called it " Spiritual Blondinism," which is another way of saying that it is a most perilous life. There must be no compromise with sin. We must never listen to its entreaties.

Sin not Sins. It is difficult to exaggerate the importance of this chapter. So far in this Epistle we have learned that we are free from guilt. How are we to use that freedom ? What kind of life must the justified live ? Freed from the burden of guilt, am I to live in bondage to sin ? This chapter decisively says, " No."

Observe the question now being dealt with is not the question of *sins* (evil actions), but the question of *sin* (evil nature) ; not with the *fruits* of the evil tree, but with the *evil tree itself* ; not what we have done, but what we are.

Deliverance from Servitude. This chapter declares that the believer may have deliverance from the servitude of sin.

Death of the Slave. The amazing thing about this deliverance is that it comes not through the death of the master, but the death of the slave. " It is a death into which we are brought in virtue of the death of Christ."

Dead Already. To say that we ought to die to sin is well meant, but it is not the truth. The fact is, we *are* dead ; and He will make it real in our experience if we ask and trust Him.

Other Renderings. Observe, " old man " is in 20 C. " old self ; " "body of sin " is in W., " our sinful nature ; " instead of " is " in verse 6, R.V. gives " was ; " " destroyed " means " done away," " cancelled," " paralysed," " made powerless." " We died," verse 6, R.V.

FOUR RECKONINGS

I. TWO OF GOD'S RECKONINGS

1. Concerning His Son and Sin   ..   2 Cor. 5. 21
2. Concerning the sinner and righteousness ..   ..   Gen. 15. 6

II. THE BELIEVER'S TWO RECKONINGS

1. Concerning sin   ..   ..   ..   verse 11
2. Concerning God   ..   ..   ..   verse 11

Divine Reckoning. God's thoughts are not ours, neither His method of reckoning as man's. For instance, we put the letter O, which stands for nothing, under the figure 1, and according to man's reckoning it is still 1, but God makes 2 of it—my NOTHING put under Christ's EVERY-THING, and what a change !

Influence of Thought. It is a vital matter how we reckon ourselves up. Our private thoughts about ourselves have far reaching issues. It is a law in life that our character never rises higher than our thoughts : " As a man thinketh in his heart, so is he." The thought that I make of myself is the thought that makes me.

Counted as Sin. The Lord Jesus had no sin, yet He was counted sin for us. God counted Him as sin.

Counted Righteous. Abraham had no righteousness, yet because of his faith, God counted him righteous.

Dead to Sin. The believer is dead, died in Christ, and he must regard himself as such, and this is " a calculation based on fact." " But sin is not dead to me," you say. Quite so. The Apostle does not say that sin is dead to you, but that we in Christ are dead to it, and that we are to keep on reckoning this to be so. Note the present tense, Rotherham's version is, " Be reckoning." SIN WILL RING UP YOUR SOUL, BUT YOU ARE TO BE AS THOUGH YOU ARE DEAD AND NOT REPLY.

Dead to the World. A reckoning of the believer concerning God. Become absorbed in God, and you will be dead to the enticements of the world.

YIELDING

A Study on the Surrender of the Will

I. AN ASSUMPTION
We possess the power of yielding or resisting, vv. 12, 13

II. AN EXHORTATION
Refuse to yield to sin by yielding to grace .. verse 13

III. A DECLARATION .. .. ,, 14

IV. AN INQUIRY .. .. ,, 15

V. A PROTEST .. .. ,, 15

VI. A PRINCIPLE
You become servants to those you yield to ,, 16

VII. A THANKSGIVING
" Ye were," " Ye have obeyed " .. .. vv. 17, 18

VIII. AN APPLICATION .. .. vv. 19-22

Three Important Questions are asked in this chapter.
1. Shall we continue in sin *that grace may abound* ? (verse 1).
    Answered by the declaration that we died to sin in Christ
2. Are we to practice sin *because grace does abound* ? (verse 15).
    Answered by declaring the power of the human will.
3. What fruit had we in the old life ? (verse 21).
    Answered by declaring its deadly bitterness (see Study 31).

A Twofold Assumption. In verses 12 and 13 we have a twofold assumption :
1. That sin is entrenched in us, that there is an evil nature within.
2. But, as through Christ it has no claim upon us, we have the power of refusing to surrender.

Actual Salvation. Our actual salvation began when we surrendered to Divine influence and power, and progresses in proportion to the constancy and completeness of that surrender.

Mould of Doctrine. For " that *form* of doctrine " Rotherham gives " *mould* of doctrine," a very suggestive rendering.
It is (1) not the believer moulding the doctrine, but the doctrine moulding the believer. (2) Not the believer holding the doctrine, but the doctrine holding him ; and (3) the teaching was as definite in outline as a mould (nothing hazy or vague about it). (4) And the teaching was a mould designed to fashion men's lives.

THE WAGES OR THE GIFT

A man may merit Hell, but he cannot merit Heaven

I. THE SERVICE OF SIN

1. Is an **inherited** service .. .. .. vv. 17-20
2. Is a **deceptive** service .. .. vv. 17-20
3. Is both a **quick** and **deferred payment** service .. vv. 21, 23
4. Is a **tyrannical** service

II. THE SERVICE OF RIGHTEOUSNESS

1. Is a service for the emancipated .. .. verse 18
2. Is a Divine service .. .. ,, 22
3. Is a Holy service .. .. vv. 19, 20
4. Is a service with a glorious yet unmerited
   ending .. .. verse 23

Wise Admonition. (Verse 21.) What did you get in your service to sin ? Unfortunately the slaves of sin do not usually stay to think. Oh, the imperative need for reflection !

Sin Personified. Sin is again personified, and viewed as a master. The subject of service looms large in this portion.

An Inherited Servitude. We were born in sin : it is the dread inheritance of the sons of men.

A Deceptive Service. In spite of its promises, and the pleasure in the act of sinning, oh, the bitterness afterwards.

Quick and Deferred. It is a quick and deferred payment service, for it serves out to its devotees death here and now, and death hereafter. Some workmen get so many " subs " during the week that there is nothing to draw at the week-end. Not so is the service of sin.

A Tyrannical Service. This monster " Sin " drives his slaves.

The Service of Righteousness is the service (1) of the emancipated, (2) and is the service of God.

A Holy Service. Righteousness is holy service for it means holiness in heart, life, and service.

A Glorious End. The service of righteousness has a glorious end.

Service or Wages. Why not " wages of righteousness ? " Even for the righteous, eternal life can only be a gift.

In Christ : the life is " in " (R.V.), NOT merely ours through Christ.

STRUGGLES AND GROANS

The Struggles and Groans of the Justified :
a Leaf out of Paul's Biography

I. THE LAW

1. **Dead to the Law**
   How we came under grace   ..   ..   vv. 1-6
2. **Ministry of the Law**
   How we came under conviction   ..   vv. 7-14
3. **Helplessness of the Law**
   How we can be made holy   ..   ..   vv. 15-28

II. THE CONFLICT

1. **What is it ?** Conflict between two natures.
2. **When did it begin ?** At regeneration.
3. **Why it continues ?** Presence of Spirit and the new nature (Gal. 5. 17).
4. **Its comforting message ?** Proves that we are regenerated.
5. **How to get the victory ?** Through the Lord Jesus.

A Battle Ground. This chapter is one of the most ancient of battle grounds. Many weighty verbal battles have been fought over it.

A Personal Experience. Is this the experience of an unsaved though awakened sinner, or that of a saved man ? Opinions differ. No doubt the merely awakened have an experience like this ; but it seems clear to many, the writer included, that we have here the experience of a regenerate soul, that, in fact, we have a record here of Paul's personal experience. Observe : hitherto, in the main, he has dealt with " you " and " us," now he speaks of " I," " me," " mine."

Saved from Despair. Dr. White knew an old woman over 90 who declared that she had been saved from despair a thousand times because of this chapter. In everything but this, the mere professor can imitate the true child of God. The consciousness of this inward struggle provides us with the greatest answer we can possibly have on earth that we are the children of God.

The Chapter Key. " I " is found 30 times in this chapter. This is the key. No wonder there is so doleful an experience when it is merely " I."

Old Adam Too Strong. '"Old Adam is too strong for young Melanchthon," said the Reformer ; but, thank God, he is not too strong for Christ. He will give us the victory, day by day, and all the days.

NO CONDEMNATION

I. THE THEME
My Standing (R.V.).
My State (A.V.).

II. THE VERDICT
No Condemnation (R.V.).
No Condemnation (A.V.).

III. THE REASON
In Christ Jesus (R.V.).
Walking after the Spirit (A.V.).

Beulah Land. Years ago I wrote " Beulah Land " over this chapter in my Bible, and I have seen no cause since why I should alter that title. In chapters 1 to 3 we have Bondage ; 4 and 5, Liberty ; 6 and 7, Wilderness ; and chapter 8, Canaan, the land flowing with milk and honey.

Three Great Noes. Chapter 8 is a glorious summing up and conclusion of all that has gone before. All the arguments of the foregoing chapters are summed up, and we are introduced in it to the glorious consequences which flow from that teaching. It has been well said that it begins with " no condemnation," and ends with " no separation," while in between there is " no defeat.'

Salvation or Sanctification. Opinions differ as to whether or no the phrase " who walk not after the flesh " should be omitted. The R.V. leaves it out altogether. Some have rejoiced over this omission, for, they say, " It tends to act as a qualifying clause, and throws the soul on an examination of walk as the means of certifying that one is in Christ Jesus." But this is an error, through a mistaken notion that chapter 8 has to do with our salvation, whereas it has to do with our sanctification.

Paul's Monogram. However, the above outline deals with both views. Accepting the rendering of the R.V., we note that, because the trusting soul is " in Christ Jesus," there is no condemnation for him. " In Christ Jesus " has been happily termed " Paul's monogram." Out of Christ there is condemnation.

The Flesh and the Spirit. Taking the rendering of the A.V., we get an important truth concerning our daily life. True Christians can be divided into two classes : Those who walk after the flesh, and those who walk after the Spirit. When a child of God walks after the flesh he condemns himself (see 1 John 3. 20 and 28). When we surrender fully to the Spirit of God, and follow the things of the Spirit, we have a conscience void of offence toward God.

THE FLESH

The New Law of the Spirit makes Righteous

I. THE WEAKNESS OF THE FLESH .. .. verse 3

Few things are more important to us than moral and spiritual strength. Milton, in " Paradise Lost," puts into Satan's mouth this : " To be weak is to be miserable." We can go further and say : " To be weak is to be wicked." Yes, to be wicked is both the cause and the proof of moral impotence. Here in verse 3 the weakness of man is pointed out, and the helplessness of the Law. But the Law was not in fault—it failed through the weakness of the flesh. *After all, what can a good workman do with bad materials* ! What the law could not do God has done— by way of the Cross.

II. THE JUDGMENT IN THE FLESH .. .. verse 3

This is an utterance of stupendous depth and significance. Few Christians have clearly grasped this truth and teaching. In next study we deal with this thought more fully than we could here.

III. THE VICTORY OVER THE FLESH .. .. verse 4

1. Now we are able to do in spite of the weakness of the flesh what we could not do before.

2. " *After* " the flesh or Spirit means " down towards " or " according to."

3. Some think that verse 4 refers to justification, but that cannot be. Please note—" That the righteousness of the Law might be fulfilled *in us*," not *for us*. The truth concerning " *for us* " has been dealt with in previous chapters.

4. Being justified, I am indwelt by the Holy Spirit, and that gracious and all-powerful indwelling Presence enables me to live holily, and thus meet the righteous requirements of the Law. The righteous thing which the Law sought in man but could not produce, was love (see Matt. 22. 37-39). The Holy Spirit sheds Divine love in the regenerate heart. Thus Romans 13. 8-10 is realised in the Christian's experience and life.

The Value of this Death. Paul in his writings cannot long remain away from the Cross. Here is an instance : " No condemnation." But why ? " Condemned sin in the flesh." *Sin was arraigned in the dock of Christ's humanity, and condemned.*

SIN CONDEMNED

The Fact that Sin was Condemned and Executed in the Person
of Christ shows

I. THE HARMFULNESS OF SIN

Sin was arraigned in the dock of Christ's humanity, and condemned. What is the result ? When a prisoner is convicted and
condemned, the public learn by that act of the judge that this
person was the guilty one who had broken the law of the land, and
harmed society. By that act of condemnation we learn the
harmfulness of that individual. By sin being condemned in the
dock of Christ's humanity we learn what it was that led us to
wreck the laws of God and harm us so grievously. But, alas,
men and women do not know the true identity of their enemy,
sin, else they would not call it by so many fancy names—as
circumstances, misfortune, heredity, weakness, fate.

II. THE JUDGMENT OF SIN

Sin was not only condemned in the humanity of Christ, but
the sentence was carried out. " Sin is never forgiven (sins are) ;
it is judged, condemned, sentenced, put to death, executed."
" The great difference between a believer and an unbeliever,"
writes Marcus Rainsford, " is this, the believer has his judgment day behind him, whilst the unbeliever has his judgment day
before him." What is the meaning of this ? God condemns
sin in Christ's flesh for sin in ours ; the sentence falls on sin and
not the sinner ; the sin shall perish, but not the repentant sinner.

III. THE HELPLESSNESS OF SIN

C. and H's. rendering of condemned is " Worsted it." The
sin was not only condemned, but executed in the dock of Christ's
humanity. Thus Christ's mission was not only to atone for sin,
but in virtue of that atonement, destroy its dominion. The
Cross condemned sin in us, so as to loose its hold upon us.

A Mine of Precious Truths. This verse contains a mine of precious truths. (1) *Pre-existence of the Lord Jesus* : " God sending "—the Christ was God's own Son before He was sent. (2) *Deity of Christ* : " Own Son." He stands alone in Divine Sonship. (3) *Incarnation of Christ* : " In likeness of sinful flesh." Not sinful flesh, but, *likeness* of sinful flesh. Christ's body was a real body, a real human nature, only without its corruptions. (4) *Atonement of Christ* : " And for sin condemned sin in the flesh."

" **As Sin.**" " For sin " is literally " as sin," or " in the character of sin." He not only died FOR sin, but also AS sin. Sin, as the cause of sin, is here personified in Christ, and God deals with Him as He would with it.

The Crucifixion of Sin. A young Presbyterian minister was converted through noticing this. In his diary, Monday, 20th May, 1850, he writes: " Writing lecture for Presbytery. Subject, Romans 8. 6, 'To be carnally minded is death.' Began by taking a view of the preceding verses of this chapter...little imagining what was in store for me. ' For sin ' (verse 3), *i.e.*, in its character as sin ! I see this as I never saw it before. How glorious ! I have got *such a view of the crucifixion of sin*, of its life's blood being now shed, as I never had before. I now see how His Name—the second Adam— has a most peculiar meaning. I now see how the sins in my flesh—the sins of all whose eyes He has opened—have been crucified to their very core, and deprived of all their power to condemn, by being condemned and put to death in the pure and holy flesh of Jesus. . . . I never until now saw what was meant by sin having been pierced to the heart—having had its poison taken out—by the sword of Divine justice being plunged into the Saviour's side, by being crucified with Christ—the Lord opened my heart, and the truth slid in."

Sin Personified. You will observe we have a step in advance on Col. 2. 14. Paul saw on the Cross not only another writing, but another thing. Sin is personified as dwelling in flesh. Certainly sin has made its fortress there. The flesh being the seat and origin of transgression, the atoning sacrifice was made in the likeness of sinful flesh, that thus He might meet sin, as it were, on its own ground, and destroy it. This is the deep and significant teaching of the Brazen Serpent. The Brazen Serpent is not an emblem of Christ in His sinless humanity—a serpent without a sting is, in a sense, a picture of Christ without sin—but *of sin personified in* Christ. He was *counted as* sin for us.

THE FIVEFOLD LIFE

A Study on the Life that Pleases God

I. A LIFE OF FAITH .. .. .. Heb. 11. 6
   Therefore be **Trustful**

II. A LIFE IN CHRIST .. .. .. Rom. 8. 8
   Therefore be **Spiritual**

III. A LIFE UNFETTERED .. .. 2 Tim. 2. 4
   Therefore be **Unworldly**

IV. A LIFE OF CONTENTMENT .. .. Num. 11. 1
   Therefore be **Thankful**

V. A LIFE OF PRAISE .. .. .. Psa 69 30, 31
   Therefore be **Praiseful**

A Worthy Ambition. For six years Alexander the Great had been engaged in war with Persia. Of all that vast Empire there remained but one stronghold to conquer—the Rock of Oxus—which was defended by 30,000 men, with ammunition and provisions to last two years. The rock was very high and craggy on all sides, and was accessible only by a single path cut in it. Recognising the immense strength of the position, he thought to win it by kindness ; so, before forming the siege, in a friendly tone he summoned the garrison to surrender. This the brave defenders refused to do, believing their natural fortress impregnable, and added that before Alexander could reach them, wings would have to be given his soldiers.

Enraged at their insolent remark, he gave orders for selecting from among the mountaineers in his army 300 of the most active and dexterous, and when they were marshalled before him he explained to them his plans. Pointing to a great rock that towered above the fortress, he stated that if he could only get a number of his soldiers on the top, a demonstration of his forces would be made before the stronghold, which would possibly awe the defenders to surrender and then he asked them if they would attempt this seemingly impossible task, promising them, if they would do so, rich rewards. The noble reply of these picked men was that they would make the attempt, but they would have their master know they were not risking their lives for mere mercenary motives; *they considered the greatest reward of all was the knowledge that they were pleasing him.*

Paul's Ambition. 2 Corinthians 5. 9 (R.V.) shows that *Paul's ambition was to please the Lord.* That was why he had risked his life 25 years for the Master. So there is a place for ambition in the Christian life. Is such a life possible ? For an answer we point to Hebrews 11. 5. If Enoch, who lived in dark and trying days, lived that life, surely we ought !

FOUR COUPLETS

I. TWO SPHERES
The Two Spheres in which to Live—
" In Flesh " and " In Spirit " .. .. vv. 8-10

II. TWO MAGNETS
The Two Magnets which seek to Attract—
" After the Flesh " and " After the
Spirit " .. .. verse 5

III. TWO MINDS
The Two Minds which decide Character—
" Of the Flesh " and " Of the Spirit " .. ,, 6

IV. TWO ISSUES
The Two Issues which Affect Happiness—
" Life " and " Peace " .. .. .. ,, 6

The Two Spheres. Who are the people referred to as being in either one or the other of these spheres ? Mauro declares that both are true of Christians : " There are Christians whose existence is in the flesh, who walk after the flesh, who please themselves, who seek the things of the world, who desire its honours, titles, and dignities, who enjoy its gratifications, who, in a word, mind earthly things. These cannot please God."

The Two Magnets. The point is this : seeing we are *not* in the flesh, not being in the sphere of the flesh, let us see to it that we do not get *absorbed* and *controlled* by fleshly and earthly things. Read W. on all the above verses. " For if men are controlled by their earthly natures, they give their minds to earthly things : if they are controlled by their spiritual natures, they give their minds to spiritual things," etc., etc.

The Two Minds. Burns the Poet speaks of the mind being the measure of the man. How suggestive is the application of that thought to verse 6. The mind can be absorbed in either fleshly or spiritual things.

The Two Issues. To be absorbed in earthly things has a deadening effect on the soul, and often leads, even God's people, to premature death. The minding of heavenly things means abundance of life—here and hereafter, and peace of mind and soul

THE SPIRIT OF CHRIST

The Holy Spirit is called the Spirit of Christ because He

I. RESTED UPON CHRIST	.. ..	Matt. 3. 16
II. WAS GIVEN TO CHRIST	.. ..	Acts 2. 33
III. WAS GIVEN BY CHRIST	..	Acts 2. 33 ; John 15. 26
IV. ACTS FOR CHRIST	.. ..	John 16. 12-15
V. TESTIFIES OF CHRIST	.. ..	John 15. 26
VI. GLORIFIES CHRIST	.. ..	John 16. 14
VII. UNITES TO CHRIST	.. ..	1 Cor. 12. 13 ; 6. 17
VIII. MAKES US LIKE CHRIST	..	Gal. 5. 21-23

A Solemn Text. This is one of the most solemn texts in the whole of the Bible. It is emphatic and penetrating.

Conflicting Opinions. There are various conflicting opinions about this verse. The question is : Should "spirit" be printed with a small or capital S ; is the Giver (the Holy Spirit), or His gift (the new nature), meant by Spirit ? Some spell it with a small " s " and read, " If any man have not a Christ-like spirit," *i.e.*, a Christ-like disposition, "he is none of His." But how do we get that disposition ? Only by His gracious indwelling Spirit. Surely we can understand that the third Person in the Trinity is referred to here.

The Deity of Christ. In this verse, the one Spirit is called Spirit of God, and Spirit of Christ. Paul regarded the Holy Spirit as proceeding equally from Father and from Son, thus declaring the Divinity and Deity of Christ.

Other References. The phrase " The Spirit of Christ " is only met with twice in the New Testament, here and in 1 Peter 1. 11. He is called also " The Spirit of Jesus" (Acts 16. 7, R.V.) and " Spirit of Jesus Christ " (Phil. 1. 19).

OUR MORTAL BODY

The Holy Spirit concerning our Mortal Body

I. SPEAKS REVERENTLY OF IT   .. Phil. 3. 21 (R.V.)

II. WARNS ABOUT DEFILING IT   .. 1 Cor. 3. 16-17

III. CONTROLS THE APPETITES   .. Rom. 8. 11

IV. ENERGISES THE PHYSICAL LIFE   .. Rom. 8. 11

V. RAISES IT IN RESURRECTION   .. Ezek. 37. 9, 10

VI. IS REASON FOR RESURRECTION   Rom. 8. 11 (*margin*)

Various Opinions. There are various opinions about this verse. The A.V. teaches that the Holy Spirit is the Agent in the resurrection of the body; the *margin* of both A.V. and R.V. teach that the presence of the Holy Spirit in our bodies now, is the reason why the earthly temple will ultimately be raised ; then some, and rightly so, view this verse as teaching that the body now receives energy through the Spirit. Why not accept all these views ? The above outline presses all the various views into service.

Our " Vile " Body. One of the most acceptable improvements in the R.V. is the rendering of Philippians 3. 21. "Vile" as in A.V. is a word reminiscent of old monastic views. How reverent is the Spirit's language.

The Spirit's Estimation. How solemn is the Holy Spirit's warning in 1 Corinthians 3. 16 and 17. Really, the more we look into the matter, the more sacred does the body prove to be in the Holy Spirit's estimation.

Our Travelling Dress. " Our present bodies constitute our travelling dress, and at the great appearing we shall change them into our bridal robes " (Jowett).

Gold in Exchange. Death has been described as " paying the debt of nature." " No ; it is not paying a debt ; it is rather like bringing a note to the Bank to obtain solid gold in exchange for it."

The Spirit's Claim. This frail tabernacle of clay, once so much defiled, is now precious to the Father because it is the habitation of the Spirit of His Son. As sure as you have His Spirit indwelling you, so sure will He raise your mortal body. The Holy Spirit who now dwells within us, will never let go His claim to the body in which He dwells.

DEBTOR AND CREDITOR

I. RITUALIST (debtor) **LAW** (creditor)
INCURRED by investing rite and cere-
mony with saving and sanctifying
value.
DISCHARGED by keeping the whole Law,
which is impossible .. .. .. Gal. 5. 3.

II. GOD (debtor) **LEGALIST** (creditor)
INCURRED by salvation by works.
(Never incurred) .. .. .. Rom. 4. 4

III. SAVED (debtor) **SPIRIT** (creditor)
INCURRED by the Holy Spirit having
quickened our souls, the promise of
quickening to our dead bodies, and
present enrichment and empowerment.
DISCHARGED by living a holy life.
1. As an act of gratitude   verse 12
2. As an obligation (debt), .. ,, 12
3. As an act of self-preservation ,, 13   Rom. 8. 12-13

IV. SAVED (debtor) **WORLD** (creditor)
INCURRED by being entrusted by God
with the Gospel as stewards and ambassadors.
DISCHARGED by preaching the Gospel .. Rom. 1. 14

V. GENTILE (debtor) **JEW** (creditor)
INCURRED by the gift from the Jew of
the Scriptures, the Saviour, Apostles,
and the first Disciples.
DISCHARGED by contributing to Jewish
missions .. .. Rom. 15. 27

A Debtor's Condition. The condition of a debtor in Paul's day was full
of hardship. Even we consider that a state of debt is degrading and
demoralising. Yet Paul was fond of the term. Five times he used it,
with rather different objects and results, as shown in this outline.

"**Therefore**" (verse 12). Note the force of this word. See how we are
indebted to the Spirit for (1) quickening the soul, (2) future quickening
of the body, and (3) present enrichment and empowerment. We owe
everything to the Spirit, and in gratitude we must repay Him by living
according to His law.

"**Mortify**" ("Make to die," R.V.) "through the Spirit ; " we cannot do
this ourselves.

THE SPIRIT'S GUIDANCE

The Outward Proof of Sonship

I. THE PRIVILEGE OF GUIDANCE

Guidance by the Spirit is

1. The Path to Sonship.
2. The Proof of Sonship.
3. The Privilege of Sonship.

II. THE GOAL OF GUIDANCE

The Holy Spirit Guides

1. Into the *truth* of God, John 16. 13 ; 1 John 2. 20-27
2. Into the *family* of God ..   ..   .. John 3. 5
3. Into the *liberty* of God .. Rom. 8. 2 ; Isa. 10. 27
4. Into and in the *will* of God   .. 1 Cor. 2. 10, 11

Normal Experience. In an interview George Whitefield, the great revivalist, had with Bishop Butler, he spoke of the guidance of the Spirit. The good Bishop said it was " a crime to speak so." " Sir," said he, " the pretending to extraordinary revelations and gifts of the Holy Spirit is a horrid thing—a very horrid thing." Instead of guidance by the Spirit being " a horrid thing," or an abnormal experience for the few, Romans 8. 14 proves that it is or ought to be the normal experience of all Christians. Observe—

1. No one is a child of God unless led by the Spirit.

2. No one can become a child of God except by that guidance.

3. The proof that you are a child of God is that you have and are being led by the Spirit.

4. The privilege of the sons of God is to be led day by day.

Sin of the World. It has been well said that " the sin of the world is a false confidence, a careless, complacent, taking for granted that a man is a Christian when he is not." But how clear and dogmatic Paul is.

Spirit More than a Power. The way to live after the Spirit, and mortify the deeds of the body (see page 39), is to yield to the Spirit ; and allow ourselves to be led along by the Spirit. *He becomes our Deliverer by becoming our Guide.* Thus the Spirit is more than a power. Hitherto the Apostle has spoken of the Spirit simply as a power through which believers mortify sin : now he speaks of Him as a gracious, loving Guide. Not only does He give power to lead a holy life, He also takes by the hand and leads us day by day into and in that holy life.

THE SPIRIT'S WITNESS

I. AN INWARD ANNOUNCEMENT

A testimony by the Spirit **to** my spirit (*i.e.*, my understanding).

II. AN INWARD CONVICTION

A testimony by the Spirit **through** my spirit (*i.e.*, a God-given conviction).

III. AN INWARD PROMPTING

A testimony of the Spirit **within** my spirit.

IV. AN INWARD AGREEMENT

A testimony of the Spirit **with** my spirit (*i.e.*, in harmony with my spirit).

Abba Father. Only three times do we meet with these two words : (1) First time in the Garden, Mark 14. 36. (2) Romans 8. 15. (3) Galatians 4. 6. It is the same word in two languages. " Abba " is Aramaic, the language of our Lord's childhood ; " Father " is Greek, the language of the learned. The force of Paul's use of the word here is this : In Israe lslaves were not permitted to use the term Abba when addressing their masters ; but we are urged by the Spirit to utter that term of endearment when speaking with God, hence this is a proof that we have not received the spirit of bondage, that we are God's freed men.

A Fourfold Testimony is shown in above outline.

1. A testimony TO my spirit, a still small voice within. Usually the Spirit speaks through the Word, making the Written Word a living voice in the heart.

2. A testimony THROUGH my spirit, a God-given conviction. " You have acquired a deep inward conviction of having been adopted as sons " (Weymouth).

3. A testimony WITHIN my spirit, a voice within (see Gal. 4. 6).

4. A testimony WITH my spirit, a voice in harmony with my spirit.

Paul states that the Spirit bears witness WITH (not merely TO) my spirit, or as it could be rendered, " together with our spirit."

Clearness of Testimony. It may be added that the witness of the Spirit is not always clear. The clearness of the testimony depends largely on the kind of life lived. Carnally minded Christians often have doubts as to their standing ; not so the consecrated soul.

SONSHIP AND SUFFERING

Paul mentions Suffering as the Inevitable Accompaniment of Sonship, and its great Privilege. He states that Suffering

I. IS AN OUTCOME OF SONSHIP

II. IS LIMITED TO THIS LIFE

III. IS ONE CONDITION OF HEIRSHIP

IV. BRINGS INTO BLESSED FELLOWSHIP

V. IS INSIGNIFICANT
in comparison with the Glory to follow.

VI. PRODUCES MATURITY OF CHARACTER

Twenty Years' Hardships. There can be no doubt that Paul was well qualified to speak on this subject. One who had packed into less than twenty years the hardships narrated in 2 Corinthians 11. 23 to 28, was well fitted to speak on suffering.

" I reckon." What a man Paul was for cool calculation. Ah, it is good sometimes to sit down and calmly reckon up things, especially the things of eternity. And this term proves that what he had to say on suffering was not a fresh and sudden decision.

The Weight of Glory. After having put the sufferings into one side of the scale, and the glory of the future into the other, he found the former were of no account whatever.

The New Nature Brings Suffering. Suffering *is an outcome of sonship.* The new nature implanted within brings suffering.

1. Through the strife between it and the old nature.

2. By reforming and making the spirit more sensitive, and pained at the presence of sin.

3. By changing the character, makes the Christian a mark for the butt of the persecutors.

Limited to this Life. Thank God, suffering *is limited to this life,* and at the longest time it is but short compared to the eternity of glory.

A Condition of Heirship. It is also *one condition of heirship,* for how can we be glorified together if we have not suffered together !

Brings into Fellowship. Suffering certainly *brings the sufferer into blessed fellowship with Him.*

Suffering has a Value Now. " Amos, the herdsman, was a bruiser of sycamore figs, a kind of fig that never ripens in that country unless it was struck by a rod, and then being bruised, it began to ripen. Probably there are very few of God's people that will ripen without suffering."

CREATION AND MANKIND

Paul here shows the Wonderful Solidarity that Exists between the Human Race and Creation

I. THE SOLIDARITY OF CREATION   ..   .. verse 20

II. THE FALL OF CREATION   ..   .. verse 22, R.V.

III. THE HOPE OF CREATION   ..   ..   .. verse 20

IV. THE EAGERNESS OF CREATION   ..   .. verse 19

V. THE REDEMPTION OF CREATION   .. vv. 19, 21

A Difficult Passage. This is one of the most striking passages in St. Paul's writings, and is one not easily dealt with.

Most Wonderful Lessons. It certainly suggests to us some of the most wonderful lessons connected with the universe.

A Second Adoption. Among the Romans, a man might adopt a child, and that child might be treated as his own for a long time. But there was a second adoption in public, when the child was brought before the authorities, and in their presence and in the presence of spectators, its ordinary garments which it had worn before were taken off, and the father who was adopting put on the new garments suited to the new life. This is precisely our position now, and this is the meaning of " waiting for adoption " (verse 23). Truly His adopted ones are we. But externally His sons do not differ in bodily appearance, power, or glory, from the rest of mankind ; like the worldly, they may be weak and suffer in many ways—temporal and physical. But all this is to be changed. Presently—

1. He will publicly own us as His.
2. Our poor dress (these bodies) will be changed.

The Whole Creation Benefits. Further, Paul points out here that man is not the only one to benefit from this manifestation—the whole of creation will benefit too.

A Wonderful Solidarity. There is a wonderful solidarity not only in the human race, but between the race and creation. " By its constitution, nature is sympathetic with the motions of the soul. Man acts on his environment as his environment reacts on him. The scars on the world's surface, in many cases, are directly attributable to enormous crimes." When man fell, his kingdom (creation) fell with him ; and creation is eagerly awaiting man's full restoration, when it, too, shall be fully delivered.

THE MINISTRY OF HOPE

Hope and Faith—Co-workers in Salvation

I. IN OUR PAST

" For by hope were we saved " (R.V.).

II. CONCERNING THE FUTURE

" For our salvation lies in hope " (C. & H.).

" It is in hope that we have been saved " (W.).

III. IN OUR PRESENT (A.V.)

1. Leads to purification (1 John 3. 3).
2. Leads to patience (Rom. 8. 25).
3. Cheers and inspires us in our daily pilgrimage.

Saved by Hope. Is this correct ? I thought we were saved by faith ? What a man Paul was for gripping the attention.

Justification by Faith. " Saved by Hope " is the statement of one loyal to justification by faith, and is given to those already in a justified state.

The Great Lever that Lifts the World. Hope exercises a sweet and loving ministry. Hope is the great lever that lifts the world. Rob a man of hope, and at once you paralyse the mainspring of action.

Hope Defined. Let us define hope. Hope has to do with the unseen future (verse 24). It is a God-given assurance concerning the future. " Faith appropriates, but hope anticipates ; faith looks backward and upward, hope looks onward. Faith accepts, but hope expects " (Dr. Griffith Thomas).

Three Tenses. The various renderings (consult W., 20 C., C. & H., A.V. and R.V.) give three tenses. All are right, though what harmonises with the context is the ministry of hope concerning the future.

The Past Tense. Hope had a great deal to do with our salvation. Observe, not hope we are saved, but " saved by hope." " Saved " is a medical phrase meaning " to make sound." *The first condition* of recovery is hope in its possibility. Despair often renders the skill of the best physician unavailing. So is it in the salvation of souls. Faith has no chance of doing us any good if hope has not visited us beforehand. Hope comes to us first, whispering words of encouragement.

The Future Tense. Our salvation is not yet fully realised, and is more of a salvation in hope than in active possession. Yet the prospect of future glory is absolutely certain, for He has pledged His Word.

The Present Tense. Word " saved " means two things, " to be *made* sound " and " to *keep* sound." Hope does her best to keep us sound.

HELPED IN PRAYER

The Prayer that God the Holy Spirit Inspires is the Prayer
that God the Father Answers

I. OUR IGNORANCE CONCERNING MATTER

II. OUR IGNORANCE CONCERNING METHOD

Observe the two renderings in A.V., R.V., and W.,
which comprehend both the MATTER and the MANNER
of prayer, *i.e.*, WHAT we should ask, and HOW to ask.

III. THE IDENTITY OF OUR HELPER

Our Helper is none other than the Holy Spirit Himself (R.V.). The emphasis is on the pronoun.

IV. THE POSITION OF OUR HELPER

Within us. God is not a mere spectator in this matter.

V. THE METHOD OF OUR HELPER

He works within us by giving and inspiring longings,
desires, convictions, all our own and yet His. Some
of these Divinely inspired longings are incapable of
full expression. God understands these unutterable
longings because they are the longings of the Spirit.

Aaron and Hur Societies. It is said that the saintly Edward Payson
established in his church what he styled " Aaron and Hur Societies," *i.e.*,
little companies of Christians who met at stated times to pray that his
preaching might lead to many conversions. In this way they upheld him,
and God marvellously blessed his ministry. Oh, that such Aaron and
Hur Societies may be multiplied everywhere!

The Difficulty Concerning Prayer. Robertson Nicoll declared that
" Prayer is at once the easiest and the hardest of spiritual sacrifices."
You see, true prayer is prayer in the Spirit, *i.e.*, prayer the Spirit inspires
and directs. " The prayer that God the Holy Spirit inspires is the prayer
that God the Father answers." The disciples did not know how to pray
as they ought, so they came to the Lord Jesus and said : " Lord, teach us
to pray " (Luke 11. 1). We, too, know not how to pray as we ought, but
we have a Divine Helper at hand in the Holy Spirit. We ought to remember our helplessness every time we approach God, and, pausing, solicit
humbly and trustingly His able assistance.

THE PROVIDENCE OF GOD

The Source of a True Optimism

I. WHAT WE KNOW

1. The **Fact** of its constant working on our behalf.
2. The **Comprehensiveness** of that working.
3. The **Harmony** of that working.
4. The **Beneficence** of that working.
5. The **Limitation** of that working.

II. WHO KNOWS

Those who trust and love God.

III. HOW WE KNOW

1. By the Word of the Lord.
2. By Personal Experience.
3. By God's Dealings with Others

The Glory of Christianity. Prof. David Smith writes : " The worth of a man's religion is determined by the help which it affords him in dark days. And this is the peculiar glory of Christianity that *it is a faith for the sorrowful*." Thus Romans 8. 28 is a notable verse, and few have done so much for the sorrowful as this.

Optimism. The word optimism has become one of the stock terms. There is a true and false optimism. A good optimism is built up on the Word of God ; and our verse points out the source of that true optimism.

Two Views of Life. " All things " occurs 22 times in the Bible. One occurrence is worthy of note : " All these things are against me " (Gen. 42. 36). What a wrong view of life this was can easily be seen from the story. Our text gives the right and proper view of life.

The Fact. There are many things we do not know, but here is one thing we do know. Note the present tense, " are."

The Comprehensiveness. " *All* "—the bitter as well as the sweet.

The Harmony. "Together." Note the 20 C. rendering. Whatever troubles may arise, God presses them into service for our good, hence the beneficence.

The Limitation. Good only for those who love God.

Who Knows. In his " Present Tenses of the Blessed Life," F. B. Meyer has a chapter on this verse, and he heads it, " The Keen Sight of Love." " Love is quick to catch the meaning of a hint, a gesture, a whisper. Love has an intimate apprehension of secrets too deep for words to convey."

PREDESTINATION

God's Five Golden Links of Salvation

I. FOREKNOWN ..	1 Peter 1. 2, 20 ; Acts 11. 23
II. PREDESTINATED	Eph. 1. 4, 5, 11
III. CALLED	Rom. 1. 6
IV. JUSTIFIED	Rom. 5. 1
V. GLORIFIED	Rom. 8. 17

Skimmed Theology. In his " Lectures on Preaching," Dr. Jowett says : " A skimmed theology will not produce a more intimate philanthropy." As skimmed milk has little nourishment for the body, so skimmed theology cannot adequately nourish the soul. A theology that can find no place for the foreknowledge and electing love of God is only skimmed theology.

The Battle Ground. These verses form one of the battle grounds of hostile creeds. Calvinists and Arminians have wrangled over this and other portions, until all the sweet life-blood was let out of them, and their true meaning hidden in the blinding dust which the strife stirred up. To-day we are less speculative and more practical than those of olden time.

A Doctrine of Comfort. This doctrine was intended for the comfort of His own. Note its connection with Romans 8. 28. " This mystery of election is both fitted and intended to bring deep blessing to the believing heart ; but the sad fact is too patent to be ignored, that with the vast majority of Christians it is so inseparably linked with controversy as to be removed from blessing altogether. Upon one side, the plain testimony of Scripture is tampered with, if not rejected ; upon the other, the doctrine is asserted with a narrowness which is uncongenial, if not absolutely incompatible with truth " (Sir Robert Anderson).

The Tendency to Extremes. The human mind has a tendency to extremes. Concerning this age-long discussion regarding the sovereignty of God and the freedom of man, the following statement appeared in the

Life of Faith : " *With the fatal tendency to extremes which characterises the human mind*, the ultra-Calvinist insisted so completely upon *the absolute sovereignty of God, that it was very difficult to see where and how man could be described as a free agent.* On the other hand, the ultra-Arminian— with precisely the same fatal tendency—insisted so *thoroughly upon the freedom of man and the royalty of the human will, that it was hard to see where the redeeming sovereignty of God had any recognition.* Rabbi Duncan, commenting on these wearying and wasteful controversies, bluntly declared that *Calvinism was all house and no door, and Arminianism was all door and no house.* And he was right. We know to-day that both emphases were wrong. Calvinism plus Arminianism is right; Arminianism plus Calvinism is right. Taken alone each is wrong.'

Can You Explain It ? Rowland Hill, when speaking of the doctrine of election, said : " *Here am I lost* ; I cannot fathom with my puny understanding the mystery of the Divine decrees—I can only say with St. Paul, ' *O the depth.*' I know it is my duty to invite *all* to Christ, but the Holy Spirit of the living God can alone enable the sinner to accept the invitation. . . . Why God *passes by* some and accepts others, I cannot tell. We must wait till we see as we are seen, and know as we are known. We know nothing. Can any man tell me *why* grass is green ? Then let us leave all *explanations,* and believe what God has revealed.'

For Whom is this Doctrine ? " There are hours in life when it is of the greatest possible comfort to get down to the bed-rock of His electing grace. This doctrine ought not to be presented to the inquirer ; for, whatever it may mean, it contains nothing to discourage the free access of any and every one to God. He has not spoken in secret, and said of any seeking soul, ' Seek ye My face,' in vain. Nay, for all the world the door of mercy stands open, and over it this legend is inscribed, ' Whosoever will let him enter. . . . Him that cometh to Me, I will in no wise cast out.' It is only when we have entered that ever-open door that we are confronted with another legend, inscribed in gold, and set around the room : ' In whom also we were made a heritage, having been foreordained according to the purpose of Him who worketh all things after the counsel of His own will." In other words, *the comfort and meaning of God's electing* purposes is not for those who are *without*, but those who are *within* God's home " (F. B. Meyer)

Foreknowledge. This is the foundation or first step of salvation. His Divine wisdom forecasted those who should believe, and His Divine purpose included them. The doctrine of foreknowledge lies at the very foundation of our faith. Surely we cannot conceive of God without fore-knowledge! This is the clue to the mystery of the doctrine. Election is always associated with foreknowledge (see 1 Peter 1. 2 and 20). But this does not exclude human freedom and responsibility. Study Acts 2. 23. The murderers of Christ were acting in fulfilment of a Divine decree, and yet this fell deed was really and actually their own. Fore-knowledge is a foreknowledge of what man would do, and what God would do for man. "There is a verse which casts a little light into the mysterious depths of this truth—not very far, but for some few feet—that from which we learn that whom God did foreknow He also did predes-tinate; *as though His Divine wisdom forecasted those who should become one with Jesus by a living faith : and His Divine purpose included them in its unchanging determinations*" (F. B. Meyer).

Predestination. God's decree follows God's knowledge. Pray note the close connection between predestination and holiness. They always go together. "If the beginning of our salvation lies in the foreknow-ledge of God, the end of our salvation lies in conformity to the Divine image, now and hereafter." Years ago I copied down in my study Bible this statement by Cecil Rhodes, the African millionaire : "If there be a God, *it is our place to get hold of what His purpose is, and to fall into line with it.*" May we fall into line with God's revealed will for us.

Called. The call follows predestination. The "called" are those who have not only heard the call, but have made a hearty response thereto.

Justified. Those who responded to the call are justified.

Glorified. "The tense in the last word is amazing. It is the most daring anticipation of faith that even the New Testament contains" (Denney). To Paul, the pilgrim is as if he were already in the Heavenly country.

Election is Associated with—

(1) **Union with Christ** (Eph. 1. 4).
   Christ alone is the Sphere of Election.

(2) **God's Foreknowledge** (Rom. 8. 28 and 1 Peter 1. 2).

(3) **God's Purposes of Service** (Eph. 2. 10).

(4) **God's Requirements of Holiness** (Eph. 1. 5; 2 Thess. 3. 13; 1 Peter 1. 2 ; Rom. 8. 28 to 30).

THE GIFTS OF GOD

Or the Gift that Brings all Gifts

I. GOD FOR US

1. As Defender   ..   ..   verse 31
2. As Provider   ..   ..   ,,   32
3. As Justifier ..   ..   ,,   33

II. CHRIST FOR US

1. In His Death   ..   ..   verse 34
2. In His Resurrection   ..   ..   ..   ,,   34
3. In His Ascension ..   ..   ,,   34
4. In His Intercession   ..   ..   ..   ,,   34

III. THE GIFT THAT BRINGS ALL GIFTS

1. The Comparison   ..   ..   verse 32
2. The Enrichment   ..   ..   ,,   32
3. The Condition   ..   ..   ,,   32

A Challenge. Right away we are confronted by a personal question. It is a challenge. What have you to say about all these glorious truths, and what are you going to make of them ?

Safety and Blessedness. We have here a series of questions, each of which brings out more and more strikingly the absolute safety and blessedness of those who are in Christ Jesus.

A Lyric Outburst. The style is worthy of our admiration. It is " a lyric outburst." The music is low and sweet at first, but it gathers force and power until it ends in one grand deafening outburst of triumph.

Security and Enrichment. The two primary thoughts in these verses are, first, our absolute safety and security, and, secondly, our enrichment.

Smile at Opposition. Here we learn that God is on our side, so that we can smile at all opposing forces.

The Greatest Gift. The Gift that brings all gifts. In the biography of David Hill, a missionary in China, we read that, after two years of most successful work he desired to erect a chapel at Wuchang. His father gave £500. This generous gift greatly touched and gladdened the son's heart, and he speaks repeatedly of it in his letters and journal. The father esteemed it lightly, and to a friend he said that " *the greatest gift he ever gave to China was David himself* : *everything was easy after that.*" "The greatest gift the Heavenly Father ever gave was His Son ; all else is easy after that, and *all* is given with Him. Without Him, nothing ; with Him, all things."

MORE THAN CONQUERORS

Christians are not Conquerors only, but MORE THAN Conquerors. Paul's way of describing a Grand and Glorious Victory gained in a Strange and Unusual Way

I. AN AMAZING VICTORY

Because it is victory **through defeat**, through my surrender.

II. AN EXTRAORDINARY VICTORY

Because it is victory **over self**, and self has overcome many a conqueror.

III. A SURPRISING VICTORY

Because it is victory **over consequences of defeat,** over the consequences of Adam's, and my own transgressions.

IV. AN UNUSUAL VICTORY

Because it is victory that is **certain from the beginning.** Other conflicts are not.

V. AN UNQUESTIONABLE VICTORY

Because it is victory that is **decisive.** No doubt about it whatever.

VI. A MOST FRUITFUL VICTORY

Because it is victory that is **no empty victory.** In worldly strife, many warriors achieve barren victories.

VII. A CONTINUOUS VICTORY

Because it is victory that is **not intermittent,** but present and continuous.

VIII. A UNIQUE VICTORY

Because it is victory which **strengthens,** and does not exhaust.

IX. AN ASTONISHING VICTORY

Because it is victory for the **weak and powerless,** not for the strong or powerful

More than Conqueror. Have you ever heard of any military leader becoming *more than* a conqueror ? In worldly strife this may be unknown ; in spiritual warfare every Christian IS, or may become, more than a conqueror.

Metaphor and Exhortation. There is no more popular metaphor than that which represents life as a battle ; and there is no exhortation more certain to stir our blood than the call to victory.

Sure and Certain. It has been well said that " Armies that go out without the inspiring presence of hope prepare themselves for defeat. There is what we call the courage of despair, but it lacks the very elements of victory. It has dash but no sight ; it has force but no song ; it is a wild leap, and not the jubilant march of strength " (Robertson Nicoll). We can begin the Christian fight in sure and certain hope of a glorious and radiant victory.

Every Conceivable Enemy. The question asked is not what will cause Him to cease to love us (His love is eternal), but what will cause us to cease to love Him. Every conceivable enemy is contemplated in this wonderful enumeration. But " in all these things," whilst weltering amongst them, whilst ringed about by them as by an encircling enemy, we are more than conquerors !

A Victory Through Defeat. He who is victorious through victory is a conqueror, but he who is victorious through defeat is more than conqueror. We conquer through being defeated by the Lord. When I surrender to Him I become more than a conqueror.

A Victory Over Self. The great business of Dr. Johnstone's life was to escape from himself. Alexander the Great conquered the world, but was conquered by himself and slain by indulgence in strong drink. If I conquer self I become a greater conqueror than Alexander.

Certain from the Beginning and *very decisive*, and that is more than can be said of some earthly battles.

A Fruitful Victory, rich in blessing to self and others.

Make me a Captive, Lord.

> " Make me a captive, Lord, and then I shall be free ;
> Force me to render up my sword, and I shall conqueror be.
> I sink in life's alarms when by myself I stand ;
> Imprison me within Thy arms, and strong shall be my hand."

SECTION 2

DISPENSATIONAL

ROMANS 9—11

SORROW FOR THE UNSAVED

Paul's great Grief at the State of his Unsaved Kinsmen

I. ITS UNSELFISHNESS

II. ITS SINCERITY

III. ITS SOURCE

IV. ITS NATURE

V. ITS DEGREE

VI. ITS FRUIT

An Abrupt Change. The change from chapter 8 to 9 is abrupt and striking. From heights of triumph he plunges into depths of sorrow. There you had the exulting song of the warrior ; here you have the wail of the mourner.

The Problem of the Day. This dispensational section has been much neglected by students. To view it as a parenthesis is wrong ; it is the very heart of the Epistle. It was THE problem of that day.

Paul Regarded as a Traitor. To see the force of chap. 9. 1 to 3, we must remember that Paul was regarded as a traitor to the interests of his people (Acts 21. 28 ; 22. 22 ; 25. 24). Here he proves his love.

Intensifies Patriotism. Faith in Christ does not destroy, but intensifies patriotism. Paul did not cease to be a Jew when he became a Christian ; neither do Britishers cease to become British when they become Christians.

Various Opinions are held as to the exact meaning of verse 3. Here are some renderings : Past tense : " Was wishing " (Kelly), " I used to wish " (Bullinger). Present tense : " I caught myself wishing " (Nicoll) ; indefinite tense : " I could " (A.V.).

An Unselfish Sorrow. The statement follows a contemplation of the believer's glorious position and privilege. But when he considered his state with the state of his unsaved kinsmen, he was full of grief. He could neither say nor think : " I am safe ; I won't trouble about them, for they have themselves to blame." Therefore it was an unselfish sorrow.

A Sincere Sorrow. Christ, the Holy Ghost, and Paul's own conscience, are called to bear witness as to his perfect sincerity

Its Source. His language shows that it was a sorrow which sprang from no mere natural source. He spake as a man in Christ.

Its Nature. It was a heart pain (see R.V.).

Its Degree was intense and continual—" unceasing pain " (R.V.).

Its Fruit is shown by that unparalleled desire—willing to be damned in order to save his beloved nation.

VINDICATING GOD

If Paul was Right, had God Broken His Word ?

I. JEWISH OPINION

The very fact of being a Jew entitled him to the blessings of the covenant, and to be regarded as a child of God.

This Paul denied strenuously.

II. JEWISH OBJECTION

If, as Paul taught, regeneration was essential to a participation in the covenant, and consequent on the nation's non-acceptance of that dogma, they had been set aside, then God had broken His Word.

III. PAUL'S ARGUMENT

Based on the distinction we must make between Abraham's " seed " and " children."

IV. APPLICATION

It is possible to belong to the visible Church and not to the invisible.

The Apostle's Next Step. After having assured the Jews of his deep love for them, and pointed out the great advantages they as a people possessed, the apostle's next step is to vindicate God.

An Abrupt Introduction. The subject is introduced very abruptly. He meets an imaginary, or perhaps a real objection. Possibly the Jews were then declaring that if Paul was right, God had broken His Word.

The Force of the Argument. To understand the force of Paul's argument we must notice the general opinion amongst the Jews (as No. I in above outline), and the Jewish objection (No. II of outline).

Inheritors of the Promise. In his argument we have Paul's deep love for his nation (vv. 1 to 3), and his proud enumeration of Israel's privileges (vv. 4 and 5), then the challenge accepted (" Not as though," etc.). The difference between Abraham's " seed " and " children " is pointed out (vv. 6, 7, 8, with John 8. 37 and 39). Even John the Baptist denounced the popular Jewish opinion (Matt. 3. 9). The mistake the Jews made was in thinking that God's promise embraced ALL the children of Abraham, whereas it was limited to Israel and his descendants through Jacob. Abraham had other sons—six by Keturah—yet THEY were not inheritors of the promise. The fact that Israel alone was taken into the covenant made by God with Abraham did not make the Word of God of none effect !

The Application's Importance. Firstly, to the Jew. God had a remnant according to the election of grace, and they were the true seed, and God's promises in a measure were fulfilled in them.

Secondly, to us. It is possible to belong to the visible Church, and yet not belong to the invisible Church ; possible to belong to a Christian community, and yet not to be a Christian.

THE SOVEREIGNTY OF GOD

I. THE PREMISE

1. God's will and choice are sovereign.

2. He deliberately reserves and retains His own absolute liberty in all matters, and His right to dispense His blessings where and how He pleases.

3. He never gives up this liberty of action.

4. Though sovereign, yet the Divine will and choice are never irrational or unrighteous.

5. Though His will is mysterious, it is based on reason (as Eph. 1. 5, 9, 11).

II. ILLUSTRATED AND PROVED

God's Sovereignty as seen in

1. **The Act of Selection or Election** ..   ..   vv. 10-13
2. **The Bestowal of Mercy**   ..   ..   ..   vv. 14-16
3. **The Exercise of Judgment**   ..   ..   vv. 17, 18

Repulsive. " The assertion of Divine sovereignty though a necessary truth which springs out of the very nature of God, is repulsive to the natural mind " (W. Kelly).

Divine Rights. We hear a great deal to-day about the rights of man, but little about the rights of God; yet He has His rights, too (see premise). " The doctrine which denies God His *majesty* is self-convicted of false-hood " (W. Kelly).

Illustrations. Note argument in previous study. The illustration drawn from Ishmael and Isaac clearly sets forth the distinction between the natural and the spiritual Israelite. Yet it leaves one great truth to emphasize, viz., the right of unfettered grace to be free to operate on whom it will. To illustrate God's sovereignty in grace and judgment we have the three illustrations as above.

God's Choice. After history justifies God's choice. Wickedness fore-seen was doubtless the reason for that selection.

Hated. The word " hated " means to " love less " (see John 12. 25 ; Matt. 10. 39 ; Gen. 29. 30 and 31).

THE POTTER AND THE CLAY

Hath not the Potter power over the Clay ?

I. THE OBJECTION

1. If God is sovereign, then He cannot find fault with me for being a sinner, for I am as He made me, ... verse 19

2. I cannot resist His sovereign will, therefore I cannot help myself, ... ,, 19

3. How can He find fault with me for doing what I was predestined to do ? .. .. .. ,, 19

II. THE ANSWER

1. It is absurd for man to question God's dealings .. .. verse 20

2. God has a right to do as He pleases .. ,, 21

3. Human responsibility, and Divine right and forbearance .. .. vv. 22-24

A Present-Day Objection. The threefold objection recorded on the above outline is a present-day one. Sceptics to-day raise the same question.

God's Election. In his work on Genesis, C.H.M. has a valuable note : "It is deeply interesting to the spiritual mind to mark how sedulously the Spirit of God, in Romans 9, and indeed throughout Scripture, guarded against the horrid inference which the human mind draws from the doctrine of God's election."

Fitted for Destruction. Observe that when Paul speaks of " Vessels of wrath " he simply says "fitted (*i.e.*, marked) for destruction." He does not say that God fitted them ! Whereas when he refers to the " Vessels of mercy," he says, " Whom He had afore prepared unto glory." This is most marked. The fact is, men fit themselves for Hell, but it is God who fits men for Heaven.

Vessels of Wrath.
1. EARTHEN vessels (2 Cor. 4. 7), emblem of our frailty.
2. MARRED vessels (Jer. 18. 4), spoiled vessels, spoiled by sin.
3. MARKED vessels (Rom. 9. 22), marked for destruction.
4. SPARED vessels (Rom. 9. 22), a crowning sign of mercy.

Vessels of Mercy.
1. CHOSEN vessels (Acts 9. 15), for salvation and service.
2. CLEAN vessels (Isa. 66. 20), having been cleansed.
3. EMPTY vessels (2 Kings 4. 6), emptied of pride and self-will for service.
4. FILLED vessels (2 Kings 4. 6), ready for service.
5. BROKEN vessels (Psa. 31. 12 ; Judges 7. 16. 20), to let the light shine through.
6. HONOURED vessels (2 Tim. 2. 21), ready for honourable service.
7. GLORIFIED vessels (Rom. 9. 23), destined for glory.

FORE OR AFTERTHOUGHTS

There are in the very nature of things Afterthoughts with Man but None with God. All was Foreseen or Forethought by Him

I. NO AFTERTHOUGHT IN CALL OF GENTILES

Spoken of in the Scriptures more than 800 years before the actual event.

II. NO AFTERTHOUGHT IN OUR REDEMPTION

1. **His Eternal Thoughts** : "BEFORE foundation of world," *i.e.*, Eternity.
   - (a) Love (John 17. 24).
   - (b) Redemption (1 Peter 1. 29, 30).
   - (c) Salvation (Eph. 1. 4).

2. **His Agelong Thought** : "FROM the foundation," *i.e.*, Time (Matt. 13. 35; Matt. 25. 34; Rev. 13. 8; Rev. 17. 8).

Calvinism's Vitality. Robertson Nicoll expresses thus a great thought : "The vitality of Calvinism lies in its assurance that love is not a thing that began yesterday, and may end to-morrow, but that it foreknew and foreordained, and will ultimately glorify.'

A New Scheme Devised. It has been foolishly said by some that when man sinned, God had to set to work to devise a plan of salvation, and bring forward a new scheme He had not conceived before. This is an error ; **God's thoughts about love, redemption, and salvation are eternal thoughts.**

The Rejection of Israel. It seemed as if the rejection of Israel and call of the Gentiles was an afterthought of God's, but Paul proves that it was not so, but was a firm purpose in the Divine mind which He showed unto the prophets. Why, the Jewish Scriptures actually speak of the calling of the Gentiles, and the rejection of the disobedient Jews, more than 800 years before.

Before Creation. The love of God for Christ and His people s no afterthought, but an eternal thought. Redemption, too, is no afterthought, but an eternal thought—it was in His mind before creation.

In Time. The events which occurred *in time* are noted on the outline as His agelong thought.

ISRAEL AND THE REMNANT

Paul seeks to Prove that Israel has not been for ever set aside

I. SETTING ASIDE OF ISRAEL NOT

1. Supposition 11. 1
2. Whimsical 11. 2
3. Unrighteous 9. 28
4. Total 11. 1
5. Final 11. 26

II. THE REMNANT AN OBJECT OF

1. Prophecy 9. 27
2. Grace .. .. 11. 5 ; 9. 29
3. History 11. 2-4
4. Hope 9. 29

A Serious Charge. This was indeed a serious charge that Paul had to deal with—that God had broken His Word in setting Israel aside. It was all the more difficult to deal with because to a shallow thinker it seemed to be true. But Joshua's glorious testimony Josh. 23. 14) is ever true, and all our days 1 Kings 8. 56 is also true. Dare to trust His Word in spite of all to the contrary. Paul proceeds to show that the call of the Gentiles, and the setting aside of Israel, actually fulfilled God's Word.

A Startling Climax. " Paul's second quotation from Isaiah 1. 9, brings his teaching about God's sovereign and electing grace to a startling climax. Had it not been for the mercy of the Lord of Hosts in sparing a " seed," Israel, like the inhabitants of Sodom and Gomorrah, would have been totally destroyed. The very fact of God's election of a remnant was a proof of His kindness, not His severity."

CHRIST, THE STONE

I. ORIGIN
  1. **Mysterious** .. .. Dan. 2. 34
  2. **Divine** .. .. Gen. 49. 24

II. CHARACTER
  1. **Stable** .. .. 1 Peter 2. 4
  2. **Living** .. .. ,,
  3. **Chosen** .. .. ,,
  4. **Precious** .. .. ,,
  5. **Tested** .. .. Isa. 28. 16
  6. **Reliable** .. .. ,,

III. HISTORY
  1. **Witness** .. .. Josh. 24. 27
  2. **Smitten** .. .. Exod. 17. 6 ; 1 Cor. 10. 4
  3. **Buried** .. .. Exod. 15. 5

IV. MISSION
  1. **Foundation Stone** .. .. Matt. 7. 24, 25
  2. **Stumbling Stone** .. Rom. 9. 32, 33 ; 1 Cor. 1. 23
  3. **Chief Corner Stone** .. Eph. 2. 20 ; 1 Peter 2. 6
  4. **Smiting and Growing Stone** .. .. Dan. 2. 35
  5. **Head Stone** .. .. Psa. 118. 22
  6. **Crushing Stone** .. .. .. Matt. 21. 44

Human Responsibility. You will observe that Paul is dealing here not with Divine sovereignty, but with human responsibility.

Israel's Failure. Israel had failed, not because they were not elected of God, but because they would not submit to His terms of salvation.

A Paradox. What a paradox we have in verses 30 and 31 ! The Gentiles did not pursue righteousness and yet overtook it ; the Jews pursued after righteousness, and never arrived at it. The explanation, of course, is that there was a difference in the way of seeking. The former sought in God's way, whilst the latter sought in their own way.

A Stumbling Stone. Oh, the pity of it ! Christ, intended for a foundation stone to build upon, yet becoming a stone to stumble over !

A Rock of Offence. What is He to you ? He is either the Rock on which you are building, or the Rock of offence.

Christ the Stone makes a most interesting Bible study.
  1. How mysterious His origin. Man did not cut it out of the mountain, but it was the work of an unseen agency, a prophecy of the supernatural origin of the Lord Jesus.
  2. Jesus, the Living Stone, was erected by God as a witness to His love for the sinner, yet His hatred to sin ; His witness for us, if we turn to Him, against us if we reject Him.
  3. Buried Stone. Before our sins could sink in the sea of God's forgetfulness Jesus had to fathom its depths

THE ADVANTAGES AND LIMITATIONS
OF ZEAL

I. THE FAULTY

1. Paul gave Israel **credit** for zeal.
2. They had a **jealousy** for God's Name, Word, and Worship.
3. That very zeal led them to **reject** Christ.
4. Israel's fate sufficiently proves that **sincerity** is no passport to God's favour or Heaven.

II. THE IDEAL

1. Has God for its **source**, " of God " (A.V.).
2. Has God for its **object**, " for God " (R.V.).
3. Has knowledge for its **guide.**
4. Has love for its **companion.**

Credit for Zeal. Each of these three chapters on the rejection of Israel Paul commences with a warm personal testimony to his love and pity for Israel. There are some who, when they find anything wrong with another, cannot think a good thought of them. They rush off to extremes. Paul avoided this by giving Israel credit for zeal.

The Tragedy of Zeal. But, oh the pity of it ! That very zeal led them to reject Christ. This is tragic.

A Modern Fallacy. In modern eyes sincerity covers a multitude of sins. " It really doesn't matter so long as we are sincere," is a frequent utterance and excuse for not accepting Christ and His Gospel. These consider sincerity a sufficient passport to Heaven. Israel's fate is a sufficient answer to this fallacy.

A False Charity. There is a false charity abroad these days. Remember, " toleration is a plant of easy growth in the soil of indifference." The friends of a most amiable and exemplary young Scottish minister feared (and with justice, too, as his subsequent history proved) he was not regenerated, and one of the peculiarities which used to raise the suspicion in the minds of some that there was a link wanting somewhere was his " abounding charity."

Zeal and Ignorance. A zeal for God, but not according to " correct knowledge " is R.'s rendering of verse 2. Israel were zealous, but their zeal was absolutely void of all real knowledge. Alas, the combination of religious zeal and ignorance of Bible truth is unutterably sad, and only too common.

Zeal and Love. Zeal must have love as well as knowledge for its companion, a zeal tempered by love. " Zeal alone may degenerate into ferociousness and brutality, and love alone into fastidiousness and delicacy. Paul combined both qualities " (Cecil).

CHRIST, THE END OF THE LAW

Christ has Fulfilled Every One of the Law's Demands

I. MAN'S RIGHTEOUSNESS

1. Seeking to Establish.. .. .. .. verse 3
2. Described by Moses .. .. „ 5
3. Secured by Doing

II. GOD'S RIGHTEOUSNESS

1. Israel's Ignorance of .. .. .. verse 3
2. Described by Moses .. .. „ 6
3. Submit to .. .. „ 3
4. Is a Person .. .. „ 4
5. Easily Secured

III. CHRIST, THE END OF THE LAW

1. Its Goal .. Its Aim and Object
2. Its Terminus .. Its Fulfilment

A Contrast. The apostle draws a contrast between the righteousness which comes from fulfilling the requirements of the law, with the righteousness which is only by simple trust in the finished work of Christ.

A Vain Effort. "Going about to establish their own righteousness." What a vain effort, doomed to failure! You might as well expect an empty sack to stand upright.

The Law's Goal is Christ. Such is Bishop Moule's rendering of verse 4. Christ as the atoning sacrifice for sin, was the grand object of the whole sacrificial code of Moses. The sacrifices of the law all pointed to Christ. A. Clarke says: "The law is our schoolmaster—it cannot save, but it leaves us at His door, where alone salvation is to be found."

The Law's Terminus is Christ. Christ has made an end of the law as a ground of justification, by fulfilling every one of its demands. He allows us to begin our Christian life with a righteousness as perfect as if we had perfectly fulfilled in our own person every iota that the law of God exacts.

SHAME

Deliverance through Faith from the Shame of

I.	CONSCIOUS GUILT	..	..	..	Jer. 6. 15
II.	DEFEAT	..	..	..	Psa. 25. 2 ; 37. 19
III.	WORK BADLY DONE	..	..	..	2 Tim. 2. 15
IV.	NATIONAL SIN	..	..	..	Ezra 9. 6
V.	MISTRUST	..	..	..	Ezra 8. 22
VI.	WORLDLINESS	..	..	..	2 Chron. 30. 15
VII.	BEING ASHAMED of Him and His Word				Mark 8. 38

Spare us This Shame. Such was the touching appeal of some Greeks to their King respecting the invasion of part of Greek territory by Bulgarian soldiers led by German officers. That appeal fell on deaf ears. We wish to persuade our fellow-mortals to make this a prayer to the King of kings. " Spare me this shame " (the sevenfold shame as shown on above outline), and He will verily answer that request.

An Important Work. Of course shame has an important work to perform in the spiritual realm. One has said : " I count him lost who is lost to shame." How true. Dryden finely said : " Love taught him to shame." This is particularly true respecting Divine love. Shame is a flame kindled by a conscience enlightened by the Spirit of God.   " Thy kind but searching glance can scan the very wounds that shame would hide."

The Shame of Defeat. The shame of defeat is the shame most in the minds of the Old Testament writers. Paul quotes Isaiah 28. 16, in Romans 9. 33; 10. 11. This is no misquotation. The shame in mind is the shame of defeat. He that believeth shall have no need of hurried flight through defeat, confusion, and shame.

Shamed Out of It. Mr. Johnson, in his " Tramps Round the Mountains of the Moon," speaking of the resolution of chief Tabaro to be a Christian, but the influence of his chief man proving too strong for him, remarks, " and shamed him out of his resolution." " I would often have been a coward, but for the shame of it," confessed one who did exploits for God.

The Shame of Worldliness (2 Chron. 30. 15). The enthusiasm of the people shamed the priests and Levites into consecration.

BELIEF AND CONFESSION

The Imperative Need of Confession as well as of Believing in
order to an Enjoyment of Salvation

I. SALVATION

1. **Not by Attempting the Impossible** .. .. vv. 6, 7
2. **Accessible** .. .. verse 8
3. **Apprehensible** .. .. „ 8

II. BELIEF

1. **Its Place** .. In fall and recovery
2. **Its Nature** .. Heart belief
3. **Its Object** .. Risen Christ
4. **Its Issue** .. Righteousness

III. CONFESSION

1. **Organ** .. .. Mouth
2. **Subject** .. Lordship of Christ
3. **Result** .. .. (*a*) Salvation
    (*b*) Assurance
    (*c*) Safety
    (*d*) Benediction

Salvation. To be saved we are not asked to do the impossible (vv. 6
and 7). God's righteousness is not distant and difficult, but near, easy,
plain, and simple, and therefore clear and apprehensible. It is easy of
comprehension by the heart, and ready for utterance by the mouth (v. 8).
Note the emphasis on heart and mouth. They ought never to be separated.
"The mouth without the heart might be hypocrisy ; whilst the heart
without the mouth might be cowardice."

Belief. To see the force for the place the New Testament gives to faith
in our justification note this : Distrust was the turning point in the creature's fall ; how natural, then, that trust should be the turning point in
his recovery. True faith is heart faith. " Faith must be an affectionate
exercise of my will, a living and whole-hearted faith."

Confession in My Life. Of course I must make confession of Him in
my life, but I must also confess Him with my mouth. On one occasion

Sir R. Peel was in the company of many distinguished men. The conversation gradually became hostile to religion. Sir R. Peel summoned his carriage. When it was announced he rose, and said quietly, " Gentlemen, I must ask you to excuse me : I am still a Christian."

The Subject of Your Confession must be the Lordship of Christ—" Jesus as Lord " (R.V.), not merely Jesus as Saviour. He becomes my Saviour in order to become my Lord.

Bible Confession. When Hedley Vicars found Christ, at first he felt himself too weak to take his own oral stand, so he obtained a big Bible, and laid it on the table in his tent in order that it might speak for him until he had strength enough to speak for himself. Never be ashamed to be seen with your Bible.

Confessing in the World. D. L. Moody related how in one of his meetings, after many had spoken, a Norwegian boy got up and in broken English said : " If I tell the world about Christ, He will tell His Father about me." Mr. Moody was wont to add : " That wrote itself upon my heart."

Safety in Confession. Note the distinction made between righteousness, which comes from believing, and salvation, which comes from confession. Salvation means safety as well as pardon, and the former is meant here by the word salvation.

Assurance in Confession. We realise the righteousness received through believing by confession of Christ as Lord. The more we confess and profess our faith, the more it will obtain a hold upon our own lives. F. Y. Fullerton writes : " One summer on the Swiss mountains the second verse of the 107th Psalm came home to me with power, and on my return to Leicester my first sermon was on the text, 'Let the redeemed of the Lord say so.' The whole point of the message was that our doubts would flee, and that redemption would become a more assured fact in our experience if, trusting in Christ, we said so. Since that time the thought has travelled widely, and I have seen the text often used on motto cards ; but its first use was in the heart of a member of my congregation. The words kept sounding in her heart, ' Say so,' ' Say so,' and she could get no rest until she obeyed the exhortation. Confession precipitated the faith that was in solution, and crystallised her dissolving hope."

Christ's Benediction on Confession. " I cannot help thinking that, when a man stands anywhere and makes his confession, whether it be the first confession of his faith, or the confession and testimony of his loyalty before men, in brave word and costly deed, there falls upon his spirit that benediction of Christ, ' Blessed art thou, Simon Barjona ' " (Clow).

THERE IS NO DIFFERENCE

There is No Difference in the

I. HUMBLING OF ALL .. .. .. Rom. 3. 22, 23

II. PURIFICATION OF ALL .. .. Acts 15. 9

III. ENRICHMENT OF ALL .. .. Rom. 10. 11-13

A Characteristic Phrase. This is one of Paul's Characteristic Phrases, and is only found three times in the New Testament.

True in Many Senses. " The things in which all men are alike are far more important than those in which they differ. The diversities are superficial ; the identities are deep as life. Physical processes and wants are the same for everybody. All men, be they kings or beggars, civilised or savage, rich or poor, wise or foolish, cultivated or illiterate, breathe the same breath, hunger and thirst, eat and drink, sleep, fall ill with the same diseases, and die alike."

In the Humbling of All. What a humbling statement Romans 3. 22 and 23 is ! It drags us all down from our self-righteous pedestals. Whilst there may be a difference in the degree of sin, there is no difference in the fact of sin. All blacks are not the same shade ; all sin is not of the same gravity. " God never said that all men were sinners alike, but He says that all men were alike sinners " (Dr. Pierson).

In the Purification of All. Blessed be God, there is more than one sense in which there is no difference. If there is no difference in the fact of human guilt, there is no difference in a gracious God who will extend His saving mercy to all that call upon Him. All may have hearts of purity.

In the Enrichment of All. He is " over all " without distinction, and He is the " same " to all—ready to pour out the wealth of His grace to any one and every one who seeks Him. Note the exquisitely simple terms of acceptance (v. 13).

" For the Scripture Saith." The Bible is still authoritative. " When my Lord Jesus became a living, unutterable, and necessary reality to me, I remember that one of my first sensations of profound relief was : He absolutely trusted the Bible, and though there are in it things inexplicable and intricate that have puzzled me so much, I am going ... reverently, to trust the Book because of Him " (Bishop Handley Moule).

MISSIONARY ENTERPRISE

Heralds of the Cross Indispensable

I.	**ITS NECESSITY**	..	..	..	..	.. verse 14
II.	**ITS MESSAGE**	..	..	..	..	„ 14
III.	**ITS OFFICE**	..	..	..	..	„ 17
IV.	**ITS GLORY**	..	..	..	..	„ 15
V.	**ITS DIFFERENCE**	..	..	..	..	„ 16

Perfect Logic. The logic in verse 14 is perfect. If salvation depends on calling, it follows that men cannot call on Him in whom they have not believed ; and how can they believe on what they have not heard, and how shall they hear without a preacher ; and how can there be a preacher unless the Church which holds the sacred light sends her messengers forth ?

Other Preachers. " Sun, moon, and stars are God's travelling preachers. They are apostles on their journeys, confirming those who fear the Lord ; judges on circuit, condemning those who worship idols" (Spurgeon). But these are not sufficient—God must have living men.

Ram's Horns. Old Berridge wrote to Rowland Hill when he had just been ordained Deacon : " Study not to be a fine preacher. Jerichos are blown down with ram's horns."

A Message to Every Nation. A veteran soldier was once questioned : " Supposing your King desired a message conveyed to every nation under the sun, and commissioned his army to carry that message, how long would it take ? " The experienced old soldier considered a moment and then replied : " I should say about eighteen months." Our King of kings has desired a message to be carried to every nation. Nearly nineteen hundred years have rolled by since He commanded, "Go ye into all the world and preach the Gospel to every creature," but the Church of Christ has not yet fulfilled the command.

The Glorious Message. O the glory of preaching His Word (v. 15). From the viewpoint of Heaven there is nothing on the earth more lovely than the hastening of the feet of the preacher to spread the glorious message of the Gospel.

FOUND UNSOUGHT

Found of them that sought Me not.   The Lord

A Strange Statement. "Found of them that sought me not." That sounds strange ! I thought that only seekers were finders ! Is it not written, "Seek and ye shall find ? " Here are some who find though they sought not.

Love that Prompted. Ah, it was love that prompted the Lord to seek us out, and follow us, though we sought Him not.

A Bold Statement. Paul declares this to be a bold statement of Isaiah's, and all will agree with him when they note that it has to do with the calling of the Gentiles.

Past and Present. Paul refers to it in the past tense, Isaiah (Isa. 65. 1) in the present. Both are correct. It has been true in the past ; it is true to-day.

A Holy Jealousy. The fact of the calling of the Gentiles ought to have stirred up Israel to a holy jealousy, and provoked them to embrace the Saviour. It also should provoke Christians to love, and to good works.

The Lord Lost ? Yes, the expression "found " implies that God was lost to them. You have heard of a lost soul ; have you heard of a lost God ? Some losses are misfortunes ; this is a crime. Pray, remember, man by nature mourns not over this loss.

The Lord Found. There are two kinds of finding—the casual stumbling upon a thing or person we were not looking for, and the finding as the result of seeking.

Men are Not Conscious of their need of Christ until He comes to seek them.

The Lord Manifesting Himself (v. 20, R.V.). He must be found before He can manifest Himself (John 14. 21).

Seek Him Now. Remember it is possible to postpone until too late (John 7. 34 ; and 8. 21).

JUDICIAL BLINDNESS

A Prayerful Examination of the Solemn and Mysterious Problem
of Israel's Blindness

I. THE BLINDNESS FORETOLD
   Psalm 69. 22-28 ; Isaiah 6. 9, 10

II. QUOTED AT THREE GREAT CRISES
   Matthew 13. 14 ; John 12. 40 ; Acts 28. 25-27

III. THE BLINDNESS FULFILLED
   Acts 28. 25-27 ; Romans 11. 8, 25.

IV. EXPLAINED AS DUE TO
   1. Israel's Sin.
   2. An Act of God.
   3. Judgment from God.

V. RESULT OF THE BLINDNESS
   1. Burdened with Ceremonialism   ..   .. verse 9
   2. Lack of Spiritual Perception   ..   ..   ,, 10
   3. Bondage and Weakness   ..   ..   ..   ,, 10
   4. Callousness   ..   ..   ..   see verse 10 in 20 C.

Going Cautiously. This is indeed a most solemn and mysterious problem. Let us creep slowly and cautiously.

The Blindness Foretold. This hardening or blinding of Israel was no chance thing, but was foretold, and this prophecy is written down seven times, and solemnly quoted in three great dispensational crises.

The Time. When first mentioned, the time was indefinite and secret. In Romans 11. 8, the time is revealed, and will last as long as Romans 11. 25.

An Act of God. The blindness as an act of God is explained thus : " If we place our hand in the fire we may say, if we will, that the fire did it, or that God did it, the last named expression being equivalent to saying that it was by the law of nature that comes from God. So in the moral world, when we rebel we set in motion the laws of God's universe which act upon our soul, and tend to blind and harden us."

Spiritual Judgments. Of all judgments, spiritual judgments are the most to be dreaded, though they make the least noise.

A Judicial Act. In this judicial act of God we see Him sentencing the impenitent adversaries of His Christ to more blindness and ruin.

Verse 9. Verse 9 is difficult, yet surely it means that, just whatever Israel took pleasure in, and expected refreshment from, would prove to be the means of their punishment.

THE ARMS OF THE LORD

A Figure of Speech, standing for the Lord Himself, and for
His Power

I.   TOWARD ..   .. Rom. 10. 21
1. Disobedient and Contradicting Ones
2. In Earnest Entreaty
3. Long and Patiently

II. UNDERNEATH   ..   .. Deut. 33. 27
1. Redeemed Ones
2. Purpose   .. (a) Save
            (b) Preserve
            (c) Satisfy

A Vivid Contrast. What a vivid contrast we have in these two Scriptures ! The Lord's arms toward, or underneath.

A Vast Space of Time. What a vast space of time, too, between them—quite 1500 years elapsed between these utterances.

Israel in Both Cases. And Israel is spoken of in both cases, only they had degenerated ; once they had the arms of the Lord under them, now towards them in earnest pleading.

A Figure of Speech. The arms of the Lord is, of course, a figure of speech, standing for the Lord himself, and for His power.

Toward—Whom ? Israel—" self-willed, and fault-finding " (W.) and " unyielding and contradictory " (R.) Israel. What a graphic and descriptive touch have we here.

Toward—What For ? In earnest warning of awful peril, and in earnest entreaty to fly to Him for safe refuge therefrom.

Toward—How Long ? God is depicted here as stretching forth His hands for an entire day. How trying is the holding forth of the hands only for a little while, but He does it " all day long."

To Satisfy His Love. He holds out His arms not only to rescue us from danger, but also to satisfy His great heart of love. Men and women hunger for the love of little children, and are satisfied when they are able to clasp the little bairns to their hearts. Oh, if sinners care not to come to the Lord for their own sakes, why do they not come for His sake, for the satisfying of His great heart of love ?

EVANGELIZED BY ISRAEL

Israel will be the Future Missionary People to Evangelize the World

I. ISRAEL'S REJECTION

  1. Not Total
  2. Not Permanent.
  3. Over-ruled for Good

II. ISRAEL'S RESTORATION

  1. Delayed
  2. Certain
  3. Result—Full and Final Evangelization
     of the World

The Dispensational Problem. Still dealing with the dispensational problem concerning the Jews ! Why, what has that subject to do with us ?

Paul's Gentile Readers. Evidently Paul seems to feel that his readers (for the Roman Church at that time was mainly, though not exclusively, Gentile) would think like that.

An Explanation. Verses 13 and 14 must be considered in the light of a parenthesis, by way of explaining to the Gentiles the reason for his lengthy remarks on this Jewish question. He wished to point out that all this discussion about his fellow-countrymen affected very closely the Gentile Christians.

The Rejection of Israel is pointed out as (1) not total; (2) not permanent, verses 11 and 25; and that God had so over-ruled it as to bring about the accomplishment of His purpose. Not that the Gentiles would not have received blessing if the Jews had not rejected the Saviour; on the contrary, that restoration would have meant blessing to the Gentiles.

Note the Argument. Israel's rejection brought blessing to the Gentiles, verse 11. If so much was the result of their rejection, what shall we dare to expect from their restoration ! verses 12 and 15.

Salvation of Jews. The fact is that the salvation of individual Jews now means great blessing to the Gentile world, for they become wonderful evangelists and teachers. Therefore the salvation of the Jewish nation —which is certain to take place—will mean a spiritual revival to the world.

The Most Important. At a missionary meeting long ago, when Charles Simeon sat down after speaking on behalf of Missions to Jews, Edward Bickersteth, the Secretary of the C.M.S., put a pencilled note into his hand with the question, " 8,000,000 Jews, and 800,000,000 heathen—which is the more important?" To which Simeon promptly pencilled this reply : " But what if the 8,000,000 Jews are to be life from the dead to the 800,000,000 heathen ? "

Final Evangelization. It is clearly taught in the Word, that the full and final evangelization of the world awaits the restoration of Israel.

WARNINGS TO GENTILES

The Gentiles are Warned Against

I.	SACRILEGE	.. ..	.. verse 16
II.	BOASTFULNESS	.. ..	vv. 17, 18
III.	PRIDE	.. ..	,, 19, 20
IV.	PRESUMPTION	.. ..	,, 21, 22
V.	DESPAIRING	.. ..	,, 23, 24

The Firstfruits. The meaning of verse 16 is not usually seen at first sight. The allusion is to the solemn presentation of the firstfruits, without which all the corn was regarded as unclean and unholy. The firstfruits were the portion set aside from the meal offering, which imparted its consecration to the whole mass of wheat it represented.

The Patriarchs. Who are the firstfruits referred to here ? The Patriarchs are intended, from which the people, the lump, had descended.

The Nation's Pledge. The thought here is that the Patriarchs as consecrated to God, were the representatives and pledge of the consecration of the whole nation. The spiritual glories of the Patriarchs are thus regarded as the earnest of the future which awaits the race.

The Figure of Trees. Israel is represented in the Bible under the figure of three trees—fig, olive, and vine.

The Fig Tree is typical of Israel as to national privilege.

The Olive Tree is typical of Israel's covenant privilege.

The Vine speaks of Israel's spiritual privileges and blessings.

Grafted Gentiles. The Gentiles must never forget that they have been grafted into a tree that is not their own, and that they hold their place in it only by faith. This kind of grafting may not now take place, but it did in ancient times. In olden times a wild olive was grafted on to a good but languishing olive. Let Gentiles ever remember that the Jews were the channel of blessing to the Gentiles.

THE ELEVEN MYSTERIES

I. **THE KINGDOM**
The secret of God concerning rejection of
the King and progress of the Gospel   Matt. 13. 11

II. **ISRAEL'S BLINDNESS**
The revealed secret that *partial* blindness has happened to Israel ..   ..   Rom. 11. 25

III. **THE RAPTURE**
That the Lord would come for His own
before the Judgment Day   ..   ..   1 Cor. 15. 51

IV. **THE CHURCH**
That the Church would be made up of
Gentiles as well as Jews   ..   ..   Eph. 3

V. **THE CHURCH**
That the Church stands in a most won-
derful relationship to the Lord   ..   Eph. 5. 28-32

VI. **THE INDWELLING CHRIST**
That we should know the glorious riches
of that mystery   ..   ..   ..   Col. 1. 26, 27

VII. **GOD**
Christ as the incarnate fulness of the
Godhead   ..   ..   Col. 2. 2, 3

VIII. **GODLINESS**
The secret of the processes by which
godliness is restored to man   ..   1 Tim. 3. 16

IX. **INIQUITY**
A secret not yet revealed   ..   ..   2 Thess 2. 7

X. **THE SEVEN STARS**
A secret the Lord revealed   ..   ..   Rev. 1. 20

XI. **BABYLON**
A secret not yet disclosed   ..   ..   Rev. 17. 8

The Word Mystery. Mystery is one of the words which Christianity
has borrowed from Paganism. But in adopting it, it consecrated it to new
uses by gloriously transfiguring it. The heathen religions of Asia had their
mysteries. But here was the difference : only a few were initiated into
them, whereas the Christian mysteries are secrets made known to all. The
Christian mysteries are not truths incomprehensible, but secrets disclosed
so that they may be comprehended by all. In the New Testament meaning,
mystery is a body of truth originally hidden from man's knowledge, which
man by his unaided reason and abilities would never have discovered.

Save from Self-Deceit. By verse 25 we see how profitable is a study of
the mysteries—it will save from self-deceit.

Ye Should be Ignorant. This is one of the Apostle's characteristic
phrases for drawing attention to some special and important truth. When
ever we encounter this phrase we should note it with great care.

Paul and Daniel. Attention has been drawn to a remarkable parallel
between Paul and Daniel—both of them had secrets revealed to them. Paul
is the New Testament Daniel, whilst Daniel is the Old Testament Paul.

SECTION **3**

PRACTICAL

ROMANS 12—16

THE SACRIFICIAL LIFE

We should Live the Sacrificial Life because it is

I. WELL PLEASING TO GOD
Holy and Acceptable (R.V.)

II. URGED BY THE APOSTLE
I beseech you

III. REASONABLE AND RATIONAL
Your Reasonable Service

IV. A DEBT
Our **Conscious Indebtedness** to God on account of the mercies of God

V. A HOLY ACT
A Living Sacrifice, **holy** unto God

VI. SPIRITUAL WORSHIP
It is the First Great Act of Spiritual Worship—" which is your spiritual worship " (R.V., *margin*).

VII. A CONDITION FOR FULNESS
It is One Condition for the Divine Fulness

Only the Best. When Josiah Wedgwood went the rounds of his great pottery manufactory, he always carried a little hammer, and if his critical eye detected the slightest defect in form or finish in any of his wares, he would break it, saying, " Only the best is worthy of the name of Josiah Wedgwood." Should we Christians not say, " Only the best in life and service is worthy of my Lord's Name and mine." Only the best of us, and that means the whole of our being, can satisfy our Lord. We must live the sacrificial life.

Therefore. This little word binds both sections of Paul's letter, the doctrinal and the practical. Up to this Paul has been building a massive fabric of doctrine, and now he makes the application of all this to the daily life. Doctrine and practice ought never to be divided. Men are prone to separate them, yet God has joined them together.

Three Therefores. There are three " Therefores " in Romans :
    (1) Of justification (chap. 5. 1).
    (2) Of sanctification (chap. 8. 1).
    (3) Of consecration (chap. 12. 1).
This is the Divine order—First salvation, then sanctification, and finally service.

A Reasonable Claim. How reasonable is this claim. There is nothing unreasonable about God's claim on our whole-hearted devotion.

Baptism of the Spirit. The Revised Version *margin* shows that the presenting of ourselves to God as living sacrifices ought to be the Christian's first great act of spiritual worship. Pray remember, that in the Old Testament, fire fell on sacrifices. If we desire the baptism with the Holy Ghost and of fire we must consecrate ourselves to Him, saying, " Take my life and let it be consecrated Lord, to Thee."

NONCONFORMITY

Spiritual Nonconformity, or the Influence of Mind and Thought
upon Character, and a Secret Guidance in the Will of God

I. ITS NECESSITY

II. ITS AGENCY

III. ITS FRUIT

    1. **Knowledge** of His Will

    2. **Discernment** of His Will

    3. **Approval** of His Will

    4. **Performance** of His Will

Shadow of the Mind. One is always interested in the confessions or testimonies of great men, and in noting utterances that have moulded them. Dr. A. T. Schofield, the nerve specialist, writes : "Some years ago, in the course of a sermon, I heard one sentence that I shall never forget. It is this : The mind casts a shadow just like the body. This is absolutely true, as we all know. As we pass through this world, our mind, our personality, unknown to ourselves, and without an effort or desire, is ever casting shadows for good or evil on all whom we meet."

Power of Mind. The power of thought over character and body is one of the so-called discoveries of this age. But it is an old doctrine, as is clearly seen by verse 2 : spiritual transformation by the mind. The influence of mind upon character is thus shown clearly by this Scripture.

Its Necessity. In some senses the world of Paul's day and the world of ours are different. From being a despised sect, Christianity has almost become the religion of the world. And yet really and truly the world is no different now as then : " the spirit of this age is absolute selfishness as contrasted with Divine love. Its object is the gratification of self rather than the doing of the will of God." The believer must therefore avoid taking his shape from the world around. "Be not conformed"—see to it that this is not your present state. "Do not grow" is Dr. Moule's rendering— you are not now conformed to the world, then take care of the future.

Its Agency. The foundation of all transformation of character and conduct is laid deep in a renewed mind. This is an outward transformation by an inward change. A renewed mind means a mind that is moved upon by the Holy Spirit of God and has found a change of estimates, a new set of views, and a new set of convictions. Is there not a very close connection between verses 1 and 2 ? Entire and full consecration leads to a renewing of the mind and spiritual transformation.

Its Fruit. " That ye may prove," etc. Divine guidance is a puzzle and a mystery to many Christians. It is well to point out that the chief difficulty concerning guidance lies in the condition of the inner life.

1. **A Knowledge of His Will** is the first result of the presenting of ourselves.

2. **A Discernment of His Will** is certainly the second. It is only the consecrated who can discern between what is and what is not pleasing to God. Such are prepared for loving submission in a glad

3. **Approval of His Will.** When Horace Bushnell was on his death-bed, his wife repeated to him this : " The good and perfect will of God." " Yes," the dying man replied, " acceptable and accepted." Of course such are spiritually and mentally prepared for a glad and quick

4. **Performance of His Will.**

SOBER THINKING

A Recognition that all Gifts and all Graces come from God

Surrender for Service. Observe the connection between Consecration (Study No. 70), Transformation (Study No. 71), and Service (vv. 6 to 8). To consecrate myself is no mere empty emotional act, an airy something and nothing; it is an exceedingly practical thing—a surrender for service.

Seven Ministerial Gifts are mentioned in verses 6 to 8, the first four being official, and the last three are general.

The Proportion of Faith. " According to the proportion of faith " (v. 6) is literally " according to his own experience," i.e., his preaching must not be parrot-like, a mere repetition of man's ideas, but from the mint of his own experience.

Spiritual Pride. The existence of this exhortation to sober thinking is an evidence of the danger of spiritual pride in the consecrated, especially in relation to service.

Its Magnetism. Sober thinking is magnetic, for whilst pride repels, humility attracts. Here is a strange thing—the proud are most offended by pride in others. Sober thinking means sober living ; for, as we saw in our last study, our thoughts influence our character.

Its Summons. The summons to sober thinking is for all—"every man." As it is difficult to give advice without seeming to assume superiority, note how carefully the Apostle avoids giving that impression : " I say through the grace given unto me," in other words, in urging sobriety of thought he was simply using the special gift bestowed upon him for the good of all.

Its Sanity. Sober thinking is an evidence of true sanity. To think too highly of ourselves is foolish and vain.

Its Purpose. Paul points out that the reason for sobriety of thought is the fact that there is a variety of gifts in the Christian Church.

Its Secret. The secret of sober thinking lies in a recognition that all gifts and graces come from God.

BROTHER-LIKE LOVE

The Christian's Duty to Fellow-Believers. He should be

I.	**SINCERE**	..	..	..	.. (w.)	verse 9
II.	**PURE**	..	..	..	.. (w.)	,, 9
III.	**BROTHERLY**	..	..	..	.. ..	,, 10
IV.	**HUMBLE** ..	..	..	..	.. (w.)	,, 10
V.	**UNSELFISH**	..	..	..	.. ..	,, 13
VI.	**SYMPATHETIC**	..	..	..	.. ..	,, 15
VII.	**AGREEABLE**	..	..	..	.. ..	,, 16
VIII.	**NO RESPECTER OF PERSONS**			..	(20 c.)	,, 16
IX.	**WITHOUT CONCEIT**	..	..	..	..	,, 16

Look Out for the Good. Queen Mary, after being shown through the museum of Scotland Yard, containing photographs of countless rogues, and also some of the methods, scientific and legal, for tracing crime, and for punishing it, exclaimed : " It is all very clever, but if the world were as anxious to discover and reward the good men, as it is the bad, what a pleasant place it would be ! " How true. The world, and we fear the Church, too, is full of fault-finders and critics. We want a few more on the look-out for the good in us ; we don't want to cultivate the spirit of the detective, always on the look-out for the bad. Thus we shall make life a little more pleasant for each other.

Without Dissimulation (verse 9), is in R.V. " Without hypocrisy," and in W. " perfectly sincere."

Abhor is a very strong word. " Regard with horror " is W. rendering. I must never tolerate evil. Toleration is a plant of easy growth in the soil of indifference and spiritual deadness and barrenness.

Cleave (verse 9), is literally " Be glued to that which is good."

Brotherly Love (verse 10), is literally, as Dr. Griffith Thomas points out, " Brother-like-love," love similar to that of brethren, or " Brother love," that is, love because we are brethren.

Condole and Congratulate. By verse 15 we see that we must not only condole, but also congratulate.

Worldly Honour. " In matters of worldly honour, yield to one another " is W. for " in honour preferring one another " (verse 10).

Little Faults. Note W. and 20 C. on verse 16, "Little faults in a character ought not to cause us to condemn that character," wisely remarks Cecil.

BUSINESS DEALINGS

The Christian's Duty to his Business.   In all Business Dealings
see to it that you are

I.	DILIGENT	.. ..	" Not slothful "
II.	SPIRITUAL	.. ..	" In spirit "
III.	GLOWING ..	.. ..	" Fervent "
IV.	SINGLE-EYED	.. ..	" Serving the Lord "
V.	HONEST ..	.. ..	" Providing things honest "
VI.	ATTRACTIVE		

Business.   The word " business " has a very wide application.   Though primarily it has to do with our earthly employment, it has also to do with our spiritual service.   We ought to be business-like in our Christian service.

Toil is Glorified.   Heathen religions looked upon work as degrading. Cicero, the Roman, wrote : " The occupations of all artizans are base, and the shop can have nothing of the respectable."   Christianity talks altogether in a different strain.   The very glory of Christianity is that toil is glorified.

Diligence.   It is said that one day, as Thomas Carlyle was walking in the park, a young man stopped him and said : " Mr. Carlyle, will you give a young man a motto for his life ?"   The philosopher stood still for a moment, and then replied : " Whatsoever thy hand findeth to do, do it with thy might."   Yes, diligence in earthly service is a religious duty.

Spirituality.   It is not sufficient to attend to my business, much less to allow business to predominate.   Let the spiritual control, permeate, and fuse the natural.

Fervency.   " Glowing " is another version for " fervent."   It is literally " Be boiling."

Single-eyed.   My Christian brother, for whom do you work ?   Oh, Messrs. ——.   Let me ask you again that question :   For whom do you work ?   Should it not be :   For the Lord, at Messrs. ——!   " Serving the Lord."

Honesty.   This is an old lesson, but so important.

Attractive.   " Provide things beautiful," is another version.   The need of working in an attractive and a winsome manner is here enforced.   " Be not weary in beautiful doing," is another version of a well-known verse.

PATIENT IN TRIBULATION

The Christian's Duty in Sorrow and Affliction

I. THE DUTY
Joyfulness

II. THE ENABLING
1. Hope
2. Contemplation
3. Faith
4. Prayer

III. THE RESULT
Patience

Rejoice Alway. It is a Christian's duty to be joyful and cheerful. "Rejoice in the Lord alway;" and, lest we might think Paul really did not mean what he said, he adds, "and again I say, rejoice."

Temperament. Is not this a matter of temperament and of circumstances? True, some have sunny dispositions, and naturally are light hearted; but whatever our disposition or circumstance, our duty is to be joyful.

Hope. The Christian's life ought to be joyful because it is hopeful. But how is it that all Christians are not joyful though all have good hope through grace?

Contemplation. The joy comes at the contemplation of our future prospects. Oh, think more of the glory to follow! We must live with our minds occupied with the future.

Faith. There is a great and glorious destiny for every Christian, and for such training is required. Dr. Schofield writes: "Some two years ago I had two nurses taking care of a very troublesome case, where the patient was most trying. They came to me saying they could not bear it, and must give notice. I pointed out to them the patient was educating them, and that so far from grumbling, such a training was worth their paying for. They saw my meaning, took up the work from a different point of view, viz., that of their own education, and from that time they would feel, when the patient was sweet-tempered, that they had learnt no lesson that day. The sufferings of earth form part of a complete and comprehensive training for a future so great and glorious that neither language nor thought can comprehend it."

Prayer. Our lives will be joyful in proportion as they are prayerful.

Patience. The result—life, if full of joyful hope, will be patient.

GOOD FOR EVIL

The Christian's Duty to his Enemies

I. THE TONGUE
Should speak well of　..　..　..　.. verse 14

II. THE MIND
Should wish no harm　..　..　..　..　,, 14

III. THE DISPOSITION
Should be peaceable　..　..　..　..　,, 18

IV. THE MOUTH
Should be shut in silence to wrath　..　..　,, 19

V. THE HANDS
Should care for ..　..　..　.. vv. 17, 20, 21

A Timely Exhortation. How timely this exhortation is—we have national and personal enemies.

Bless (verse 14) means " to speak well of." It has the same meaning as the word " eulogise." We are actually to talk lovingly about our enemies; we are to think and speak of their good qualities.

Curse not (verse 14) means " to wish not a curse against." Thus we are not to have even an inner and unexpressed hard feeling or wish against an enemy.

A Peaceable Disposition. We have to have a peaceable disposition (verse 18). The impossibility of this in some cases is hinted at, to keep up the hearts of those who, having tried their best, but unsuccessfully, to live in peace, might be tempted to think the failure was necessarily owing to themselves. There is such a thing as an ignoble peace, a peace at any price. Cromwell once said : " Peace is only good when we receive it out of the Father's hand, and most dangerous to go against the Will of God to attain it." Fidelity to truth often rouses the untruthful ; and fidelity to holiness and purity often enrages the unclean.

Give Place (verse 19). Stand at one side, and let wrath fly past unresisted. Do not take the law into your own hands.

Repaying. Do not pay enmity " with enmity "—treat kindly and lovingly. Remember—

Good for good is **man-like.**　　　Evil for good is **devil-like.**
Evil for evil is **beast-like.**　　　Good for evil is **God-like.**

CIVIL OBEDIENCE

The Christian's Duty to King and Country

Duties to the World. From dwelling upon our duties to our fellow-Christians and to our enemies, Paul now speaks of our duties to King and Country. Though not of the world, yet we have relative duties to it.

Holy Wisdom. Commenting upon this, W. Kelly draws attention to the holy wisdom of Paul : " By a gradual transition we are brought from not avenging ourselves, and overcoming evil with good as becomes the children of God, to our relations to the authorities in the world whose office is to avenge evil, punish evil-doers, and praise those that do well."

The Jews' Turbulence. It is important to note that the Jews at Rome were notorious for their turbulence. Their theocratic ideas of government made submission to government by Gentiles intolerable. They had lately rebelled and suffered expulsion (Acts 18. 2), hence the timeliness of this exhortation.

The Principle. The principle underlying civil obedience : " For there is no power but of God." Government rule derives its source and sanction from God Himself. Society needs government. God intends man to live under authority. Resistance to civil authority is condemned as equivalent to resistance to God Himself.

Conscience Sake. The limitations to our obedience : " For conscience sake " (verse 5). There must be obedience except when obedience would be sin. This clause about conscience leaves the Christian to witness against the State if it should invade the realm of conscience.

Paying Taxes. Duties following civil obedience—verses 6 and 7. Paying taxes is just as Christian a duty as praying.

THE PAYMENT OF DEBT

The Christian's Duty to His Fellow-Citizens

I. DEBTS THAT CAN BE PAID

To discharge all financial and other debts that ought and should be paid

1. How to be able
(a) Frugality
(b) Supplication

2. How to do it
(a) Promptly
(b) Cheerfully

II. DEBT THAT CANNOT BE PAID

To attempt daily to discharge the debt of love that cannot be paid

1. Love as a debt
(a) Not a mere emotion
(b) Honourable debt
(c) Contracted on account of another

2. How discharged
(a) By loving
(b) Showing love by conduct

No Man. " Owe no man (not merely Christians) anything, except the loving one another " (Bishop Moule's rendering).

Anything. Observe " anything "—how inclusive : either money or promises.

Men Judge Christians. This is a test men of the world apply to Christians. " Men judge Christians by their promptness in fulfilling obligations, and in paying their bills, and it is a fine, natural, and legitimate test."

Love as a Debt. By speaking of love in this way, we see that love is a duty, and not a mere emotion in which we may indulge or not as we please. Love is a duty, and thus we are bound to love.

Payment by Love. One way of paying the debt of love is by loving. No man gets his due from us except he gets love.

THE ARMOR OF LIGHT

The Christian's Duty in View of the Near Approach of the Lord's
Second Advent, is to

I. OBSERVE
The Signs of the Times ..   .. verse 11

II. DISPENSE
With Spiritual Langour..   ..   ..   ..   ,, 11

III. RECOGNISE
The Threefold Nature of Salvation ..   ..   ,, 11

IV. REMEMBER
His Coming means the Inauguration of the
Perfect Day   ..   ..   ,, 12

V. WALK BECOMINGLY
1. **By Renouncing Sins** ..   ..   ,, 13
   (a) Sins of Intemperance—Public sins
   (b) Sins of Impurity—Private sins
   (c) Sins of Discord—Social sins
2. **By Making no Forethought for Sin**   ..   ,, 14
3. **By Exhibiting Christ in Outer Life** ..   ..   ,, 14

Conversion of Augustine. These verses are memorable as connected
with the conversion of the great Augustine. He had lived a wild life,
though the child of a godly mother. Seriously impressed by the conversion of some rough Roman soldiers, he was seated in his garden, when he
heard a voice (probably the voice of children playing), repeating several
times, " Take up and read." He took up a copy of the Epistles which
lay open by his side, and the above verses first met his gaze.

The Great Incentive. Here we have the great incentive to holy living
and devoted service. The Lord's near advent is given as the reason why
we should perform all the duties mentioned, such as paying our debts,
loving others, etc., etc.

Knowledge of Instruction. An authority has pointed out that in the
Greek the knowledge referred to in verse 11 is not the knowledge of in-
tuition but of instruction—a knowledge that comes from observation, and
from the study of the Bible.

Awake out of Sleep. These words are addressed to Christians, and therefore apply not to spiritual death, but to spiritual langour. Be alert !

Salvation is spoken of in the New Testament in three tenses : (a) Past
(2 Tim. 1. 9) ; (b) Present (Acts 2. 47 ; Rom. 8. 24).; (c) Future (Acts 15.
11 ; Rom. 13. 11).

Walk Honestly is literally " walk becomingly."

DOUBTFUL THINGS

The Christian's Duty to his Weaker Brethren

I. THE DIFFICULTY

1. About food   ..   .. verse 2
2. About feasts ..   .. ,,   5

II. THE DUTY

1. Welcome into fellowship   ..   ..   ..   ,,   1
2. Associate with   ..   ..   ,,   1
3. Do not dispute with ..   ..   ,,   1
4. Do not despise or condemn   ..   ..   ,,   3
5. Do not be selfish   ..   ..   ..   chap. 15. 1
6. Seek his edification ..   ..   ..   ,,   2

III. THE REASON WHY

1. Because of God's example ..   ..   .. verse 3
2. Because of God's ownership   ..   .. ,,   4
3. Because there is a place for Christian
       individualism   ..   .. ,,   5
4. Because of Christ's example   ..   chap. 15. 3

Hyper-sensitive. Christian love has been enforced in previous chapters ;
now it is shown how it can and must be applied to a special case. The
weak in faith referred to was not one indulging in sin, but one who thought
he was sinning by not keeping certain feasts, etc.—hyper-sensitive souls,
so fearful of sin that they were needlessly burdened—they were Christians
who were still shackled in conscience by their old ritual.

Ritual and Practice. The Church at Rome was made up of Gentile and
Jewish Christians, and it is only to be expected that conflicts should arise
concerning ritual and practice.

The Cold Shoulder. The weak brother was to be welcomed into fellowship, and loved rather than argued out of his difficulties ; he was to be
associated with (" Receive . . . as a friend," W.), and no cold shoulder to
be given him ; he was not to be disputed with. We surely have something more pressing to do than criticise one another.

On His Knees. Every man must think for himself on his knees.

PERSONAL INFLUENCE

The Christian's Influence upon Others

I. A FACT CONCERNING SELF

Unconscious Influence   ..   ..   verse 7

II. A FACT CONCERNING CHRIST

And our Life and Death   ..   ..   ..   vv. 8, 9

Prosaic Settings. It is most noticeable that we have often in the New Testament great truths stated in connection with common and prosaic duties. So here we see great truths concerning personal influence and the death of Christ, and our death, spoken of in relation to meats and drinks.

Liveth to Himself. Count Zinzerdorf gave to the members of the religious body (Moravians), which he founded, a seal-ring with the words engraved upon it in Greek, " None of us liveth to himself."

Unconscious Influence. We all have an influence—an invisible something which radiates from our personality, from our inmost being. A person enters a room full of people—at once the moral and spiritual temperature either rises or falls as the result of his presence.

Across the World. The fluttering of an insect's wing is felt at the other side of the world, so scientists declare. This fact lends dignity and value to our lives.

Solitary Confinement is the worst of all punishments. Those who " live to self " inflict this punishment upon themselves.

Both Worlds. Jesus died and rose again. Thank God for these facts. But why ? For one thing, that He might be Lord in both worlds. We are subjects of earthly kings while we live, but they hold no empire over the dead. Death makes no alteration in our relationship to the Lord. Even in death the believer is conscious of his relation to his Lord.

The Absolute Dispenser. But more than that—He, being Lord, is the absolute Dispenser of the time and manner of our dying.

THE SEVEN JUDGMENTS

I. THE JUDGED
1. Believers' Sin
2. Believers' Life, under the Word
3. Believers' Works
4. Living Nations
5. Israel
6. Angels
7. Unconverted Dead

II. THE PLACE
1. At the Cross
2. At the Throne of Grace
3. At the Reward Seat
4. On the Earth
5. In the Wilderness
6. In Heaven
7. At the Great White Throne

III. SCRIPTURE
1. John 12. 31, with 5. 24
2. 1 Corinthians 11. 31
3. Romans 14. 10 ; 2 Corinthians 5. 10
4. Matthew 25. 32 ; 1 Corinthians 6. 2
5. Ezekiel 20. 37
6. Jude 6 ; 1 Corinthians 6. 3
7. Revelation 20. 11 and 12

Accountability. That great American thinker, Daniel Webster, was once asked what was the greatest thought that ever occupied his mind, and he replied : "My personal accountability to God." That is indeed a great thought on a solemn subject. Each one of us will have to render an account to God. We are responsible beings.

The Judgment Day. Not so long ago Christian people generally saw nothing ahead but the judgment day. Then they discovered that the Millennium will precede the last day of judgment. Then, instead of the Millennium ushering in the Lord, the Lord must come first and usher in the Millennium.

The Judgment Seat. Only twice in the New Testament is the phrase, "The judgment seat of Christ," to be met with, and in both cases only addressed to believers. In Romans 14. 10, it is used in connection with treatment of brethren, and in 2 Corinthians 5. 10, it is given as one reason why the Apostle had made pleasing God the ambition of his life.

PERSONAL LIBERTY

The Limits of Personal Liberty

I. SELF-JUDGMENT
Judge yourself, and not another .. .. verse 13

II. STUMBLING BLOCKS
Avoid conduct that would lead others to stumble, much less fall .. .. .. „ 13

III. KNOWLEDGE GIVES PERCEPTION—
Paul identifies himself with the stronger one .. „ 14

IV. CLEAN IS CLEAN
A clean thing is considered unclean by the man who thinks it is so .. .. vv. 14, 20

V. WALKING CHARITABLY
Conduct, no longer controlled by love, defined verse 15

VI. LIBERTY NOT LICENSE
Liberty must not lose its good name .. .. „ 16

VII. INDULGENCE DESTRUCTIVE
Overthrowing the work grace has reared .. „ 20

VIII. SELF-DENIAL
A great and ennobling conclusion .. .. „ 21

A Notable Principle. These verses are notable. Here is enunciated a principle that has led thousands to abandon habits, amusements, and practices, for the sake of the weak.

Criticise Yourself. If you must judge, criticise yourself and not another (verse 13).

Ceremonial Distinctions. Verses 14 and 20 have reference to ceremonial distinctions of right and wrong, and not the eternal moral distinctions of right and wrong.

Stumbling. No Christian is blameless if he voluntarily acts so as to lay a stumbling block, or an occasion of stumbling, in another's way (verse 15).

Liberty or License. Liberty must not degenerate into license (verse 16).

Self-denial. There is no self-denial deserving of the name that is not willing to give up any privilege of the palate or passion, rather than endanger the least of God's children (verse 21).

THE THREE KINGDOMS

I. THE KINGDOM OF THE SON
The **Spiritual Rule** of the Son of God ..   Col. 1. 13

II. THE KINGDOM OF HEAVEN
The **Earthly Rule** of the Son of God ..   Matt. 3. 2

III. THE KINGDOM OF GOD
1. Moral—The **Spiritual Rule** of the
   Spirit of God now   ..   ..   Rom. 14. 17

2. Dispensational—The **Universal Rule**
   of the Father ; yet future   ..   1 Cor. 15. 24

Christian Living. We often limit the idea of service to Christian work ; here in verse 18 it includes Christian living. "He that in these things serveth Christ," *i.e.*, he who renders to God a service of work backed up by a service of life is pleasing to his God, and is pleasing to man.

Much Confusion exists in the minds of many Christians on the Kingdom question.

The Kingdom of the Son is the present spiritual sway over hearts and lives by the Son of God.

The Kingdom of Heaven is the Messianic earth-rule of the Lord Jesus. It is called Kingdom of Heaven because it is the rule of the Heaven over the earth. It is really the earthly sphere of the Kingdom of God.

The Kingdom of God considered morally and dispensationally—
   MORALLY. It is the spiritual rule of the Spirit of God.
   (a) Negative. Not eating and drinking. A Christian is not merely one who does not eat or drink certain things.
   (b) Positive. It is within you (Luke 17. 21), the Spirit's rule within (Rom. 14. 17).
2. DISPENSATIONALLY. It is the universal rule of God (1 Cor. 15. 24), not yet fully realised, but certain and sure.

THE NATURE OF SIN

Much Depends upon a Right Conception of Sin

I. TRANSGRESSION
Stepping over the Law of God .. 1 John 3. 4

II. UNRIGHTEOUSNESS
Coming short of the Law's requirements 1 John 5. 17

III. FAILINGS
Not living up to the light we have .. James 4. 17

IV. FAVOURITISM
Respect of persons ..   ..   .. James 2. 9

V. THOUGHTLESSNESS
Lies in the realm of thought ..   .. Prov. 24. 9

VI. HAUGHTINESS
Lies in the realm of affections ..   .. Prov. 21. 4

VII. MISDEEDS
Every action of the unsaved ..   .. Prov. 21. 4

VIII. DOUBTFULNESS
Doing doubtful things ..   ..   .. Rom. 14. 23

A Right Conception. The subject of sin is a vastly important one ; and much depends upon a right conception of it. For one thing, the Cross can only be fully understood through recognising something of sin's nature. It is only through the Word of God that we begin to understand something of the awfulness of sin.

Faith in verse 22 is used here in a somewhat unusual sense—it means convictions and settled judgments, which are the fruits of a strong faith.

A Message to the Strong One (verse 22)—

1. Will your broader views stand the searching light of His presence ? " Before God."
2. Are your broader views convictions of faith, or only inclinations ? " Hast thou faith ? "
3. Do not make a parade of your enlightened convictions. " Have it to thyself."

A Message to the Weak One (verse 23)—

1. Happy is the man whose practice does not go beyond his convictions (verse 22). "Happy is he that condemneth not," etc., etc (note W.).
2. Do not do anything you are not sure to be right.
3. If you have any doubts, the safest course is to abstain from the conduct in question.

GLORIFYING GOD

God has been and can be Glorified by

I. SAINTS BEING LIKE-MINDED

When His people are like-minded, and one in
purpose .. .. vv. 5, 6

II. SINNERS BEING RECEIVED

By Christ's welcome to us .. .. .. verse 7

III. GENTILES BEING BLESSED

God glorified by blessing bestowed to Gentiles through Christ's exclusive ministry
to the Jews .. .. vv. 8, 12

The God of Patience. What a suggestive title is " The God of patience
and consolation ! " He is worthy of it. It means that patience and consolation are His property, that He exercises it, and bestows it through the
Word (see verse 4).

Who is the God we should glorify ? None other than the Father of the
Lord Jesus.

Associate Ourselves. We have to do more than forgive each other ; we
have to associate with one another (verse 7).

Strong and Weak. In chapter 14, verse 1, Paul exhorted the strong to
receive the weak, but here he exhorts the strong and the weak to receive
each other. And why ? Because Christ has welcomed us. And if that
welcome of His glorified the Father, our welcome to one another will also
glorify the Father.

Reaching all Nations. During our Lord's earthly ministry His work
was restricted to the Jews. By concentrating His work on Israel He was
able to reach all nations.

The Gentiles Blessed.
1. Messiah praising God amidst Gentiles (verse 9).
2. Gentiles exhorted to unite with Jews in praising God (verse 10).
3. God's purpose to introduce the Gentiles into His worship (verse 11).
4. Messiah to be King over Gentiles (verse 12).

THE IDEAL LIFE

Paul's Conception of the Ideal Christian Life

I. THE SOURCE
   The God of Hope
      A life lived in direct contact with God

II. THE MEASURE
   Fill you
      A life neither starved not straitened

III. THE CHARACTER
   With all joy and peace
      A life that is bright and beautiful

IV. THE CHANNEL
   In believing
      A life that is a life of faith

V. THE PURPOSE
   That ye abound in hope
      A life overflowing with the heavenly hope

VI. THE SPHERE
   Through the power of the Holy Ghost
      A life lived in the power of the Holy Ghost

A Remedy for Controversy. This is how Paul closes his exhortation to unity : It points to the true remedy for religious controversy—fill the contending parties with a fuller spiritual life, and the ground of their differences will begin to dwindle and look very contemptible.

An Acknowledgment. For this study I am indebted to two Outlines by well-known scholars, viz., One on **Blessing,** by Dr. Griffith Thomas ; and one on **Paul's Ideal Christian Life,** by Dr. Handley Moule.

PAUL'S AMBITIONS

He Explains His Own Motives and Intentions

I. TO PLEASE GOD

We are ambitious ... to be well-pleasing

unto Him   ..   .. 2 Cor. 5. 9, R.V.

II. TO LIVE A QUIET LIFE

A quiet, peaceable, and industrious

life ..   .. 1 Thess. 4-11, R.V.

III. TO LABOUR IN FRESH FIELDS

Being ambitious to preach, etc.   .. Rom. 15-20

Motives Explained. The Epistle proper is now closed. From exhortation Paul passes to explanation. He explains his own motives and intentions. You will observe that this Epistle closes as it opens, viz., with personal commendation and explanation (see verses 1, 8, and 13).

The Model Servant. Paul's courtesy (verse 14), tactfulness (15), ministry (15 and 16), testimony and boasting (17-19), ambition (20, 21), system of working (22), success (23), plans (24), commission (25-28), conviction (29), request (30-32), and prayer (33).

Intelligence and Character. Note the connection of intelligence with holy character (verses 14, 15).

Two Offerings. Note the connection between my offering up of *myself* and then the offering of *fruit in toil*.

Four Titles are given to God in this chapter (verses 5, 13, 33).

Unbounding Liberality. What a commendable testimony these early Christians had (verses 26-28).

Fulness of the Blessing (verse 29).

Love of the Spirit (verse 30).

Agonizing Prayer. "Strive" (verse 30) is really "agonize."

UNBOUNDING LIBERALITY

The Unbounding Liberality of the Primitive Christians

I. GIVE GRATEFULLY .. .. .. Rom. 15. 27

II. GIVE METHODICALLY .. .. 1 Cor. 16. 2

III. GIVE CHEERFULLY
Cheerfully is literally Hilarious .. 2 Cor. 9. 7

IV. GIVE ABUNDANTLY .. .. .. 2 Cor. 8. 7

V. GIVE ALL .. .. 2 Cor. 8. 2

A Coffer and a Coffin. In reference to the history of the Christian Church, one has said : "As fast as the Church became a coffer for hoarding coveted wealth she became a coffin for enshrining a dead Christianity."

Individualism. Let us remember Churches are made up of individuals ; and what is true with respect to Churches is also true with respect to individuals. The early Church was a live Church, and one evidence of its life can be seen in its abounding liberality.

Poor Saints. The poor saints in Jerusalem (verse 25) probably were in such an impoverished condition through confiscation of goods (Heb. 10. 34) as one form of persecution.

A Good Investment. This collection was one of Paul's great thoughts at that time (Acts 20. 4 ; 1 Cor. 16. 1-4 ; 2 Cor. 8 and 9 ; Gal. 6. 10). Paul looked upon this as a splendid means of accomplishing one of his deepest purposes and desires—the union of Christian Jew and Gentile.

Discharging a Debt. Here the grace of liberality is spoken of as the discharging of a debt. There is no special virtue in the payment of a debt. They had received of the Jews. Now they must give of their carnal (*i.e.*, things belonging to our life in the flesh) things. This is a principle the members of an Assembly of Christians should keep in mind.

PHEBE, THE SUCCOURER

A Type of the Useful Christian

I.   A CONVERTED GREEK IDOLATRESS

II.   NOW A SISTER IN GRACE

III. LIVING PURE AMIDST IMPURITY

IV.   A WIDOW ENGAGED IN BUSINESS

V.   AN ACTIVE CHRISTIAN WORKER

VI.   A CHAMPION OF THE OPPRESSED

VII. A HELPER OF THE NEEDY

VIII. NOW IN NEED OF ASSISTANCE

Pass the Salt. " I have often noticed that the people who are ready to die for you never think it necessary to pass the salt," remarked a noted writer and thinker. That is to say, those who no doubt would do something great for us, forget the little common courtesies of life. Phebe was one who never forgot to pass the salt.

Ladies First. Here is a peculiar fact—that the two Epistles of Paul that have most salutations are his two letters sent to Churches he had never visited, viz., Romans and Colossians. In his list of salutations in Romans we find a lady at the head. " Ladies first."

Bearer of the Epistle. It is believed that Phebe was the bearer of this great Epistle to the Roman Church. But for this reference, she would have been unknown. And yet what a lot we can know of her from this notice.

A Gentile. Her name is Greek, and therefore she was a Gentile.

An Idolatress. Her name is a purely idolatrous one—the name of the Moon goddess of Greece—and undoubtedly she had been a worshipper of idols.

A Sister. She was a sister in grace.

A Pure Liver. Lived a life of purity amidst much impurity. Corinth was a seething cesspool of iniquity. If that was true of Corinth, then we may expect worse of Cenchrea, Corinth's seaport, the home of Phebe.

An Active Worker. She was an active Christian worker (" Servant " (lit. Deaconess) of the Church).

A Champion. She was the champion of the oppressed. Bishop Moule renders " succourer " as " stand-by " or " champion."

A Helper. A helper of all in need.

PRISCILLA AND AQUILA

Paul's Helpers in Jesus Christ

I. HISTORY

1. **Nationality**   He was a Jew, she was a Gentile
2. **Home**   ..   Rome, but they had been expelled
3. **Trade**   ..   Tent makers
4. **Conversion**   Led to Christ by Paul
5. **Removal** ..   From Corinth to Ephesus
6. **Service**   ..   Helped Apollos. Formed a Church

II. LESSONS

1. The Unerring Wisdom of Providence
2. The Fine Growth in Christ
3. The Effects of Christianity

A Splendid Eulogy.   What a splendid eulogy of this couple we have in
these verses.   If this was all we knew of this godly couple it would be
more than sufficient to give them an honoured position on the New Testament Roll of Honour.

Nationality.   He was a Jew, born in Pontus (Acts 18. 1-3) ; she was
probably a Gentile, as her name is Roman, so this was a mixed marriage.

Home.   Their settled home was Rome, but they had been expelled, and
were probably on their way to his birthplace when they stopped at Corinth.

Trade.   Tent makers.   On reaching Corinth they secured orders, and
engaged Paul, who laboured with them one-and-a-half years (Acts 18. 11).

Conversion.   There is little doubt but that they were led to Christ by
their illustrous employee.

Removal.   Left Corinth, and accompanied Paul to Ephesus (Acts 18.
18), and were left by Paul there (verse 19).

Service.   Whilst there, were a great help to a young man called Apollos
(Acts 18. 26).   Three years afterwards they had formed a Church in their
house at Ephesus (1 Cor. 16. 19) ; one year later were back in Rome (Rom.
16. 3. 5), and some time afterward had returned to Ephesus (2 Tim. 4. 19).

Unerring Wisdom.   How unerring is the wisdom of Providence.   The
Emperor Claudius thought he was having all his own way in banishing the
Jews from Rome, but it sent these two to Corinth to meet Paul, who led
them to Christ, and they, subsequently, saved Paul's life at great risk
to their own (Rom. 16. 4).

Growth in Christ.   The great Apostle and the obscure disciples had a
common spiritual soil.   Note that in one-and-a-half years they made such
progress in Divine knowledge that they were able to instruct the brilliant
Alexandrian orator Apollos (Acts 18. 24-26).

Effects of Christianity.   How hallowing are the effects of Christianity
on wedded life.   Have you noticed that the wife's name comes first ?
With two exceptions (Acts 18. 2 and 1 Cor. 16. 19) she always comes first.
Apart from grace, this would never have been allowed.   It would have been
an impossibility in a Roman or heathen home.   The grace of God lifts
woman to her proper place.

THE PORTRAIT GALLERY
A Few of Paul's well-beloved Friends

I. **APELLES**
  A sane and secure environment—" In Christ " vv. 10, 11
  A tested and proved character..   ..   .. verse 10

II. **EPAENETUS**
  Probably the first Ephesian convert ..   ..   ,, 5

III. **MARY**
  A useful Christian   ..   ..   ,, 6

IV. **AMPLIAS, STACHYS**
  Winsome and lovable souls   ..   ..   .. vv. 8, 9

V. **URBANE**
  One able to work well with others   ..   .. verse 9

VI. **ANDRONICHUS, JUNIA, HERODION**
  Fellow-sufferers ..   .. vv. 7, 11

VII. **TRYPHENA, TRYPHOSA**
  Two society ladies toiling in the service of
    the Lord   ..   .. verse 12

VIII. **PERSIS**
  A Persian slave girl toiling in loving service   ..   ,, 12

Aristobulus was probably the grandson of the Herod in whose life Christ was born. All of the household of Aristobulus were believers, but only a portion of the household of Narcissus.

Apelles. Was Apelles Apollos ? Some think so. He had been tried and tested on different occasions, but had given the highest proofs of the sincerity and depth of his religion.

Mary, probably a Jewess, was indeed a useful Christian. She showed her love in labour.

Kinsmen (verses 7 and 11) might mean that they were relatives of Paul, or simply members of the same nation. They were older Christians than Paul.

Tryphena and Tryphosa, probably sisters, and members of Roman Society.

Persis is a Persian name, so she was probably a slave.

Help from a Dictionary. With the aid of a good Bible dictionary, facts can be gleaned of the persons named in this section that will provide many entrancing Bible readings.

PAUL'S FINAL WORD

An Insertion. The even flow of greetings is interrupted in order to insert a solemn warning. The contrast is indeed striking. It is evident that false teachers had made their way to Rome, and Paul interrupts his greetings in order to put them on their guard.

The Tone of Entreaty. Note the tone of entreaty in verses 17 and 18. " The doctrine which ye have learned," *i.e.*, the doctrine taught them by Paul and other of the Apostles. They had no authoritative Scriptures as we have.

Scan the Description given of these false teachers in verse 8
1. Some themselves—are lustful and fleshly.
2. Flatter themselves.
3. By eloquence and choice language (" good words and fair speeches") they deceive.
4. Our duty is to (verse 17) " Mark." Keep our eyes on them and " avoid them "—do not seek their company.

Fidelity to Truth. In verse 19 " W." renders " obedience " as " fidelity to truth."

The Bruising (verse 29). Who bruises ? God. How ? By our feet. Notice how beautifully the name " God of Peace " comes in to suggest that even in the strife there may be tranquillity. When ? " Shortly." Method : He bruises, for one thing, by filling us with joy and peace.

PAUL'S DOXOLOGY

I. ESTABLISHMENT

1. **Author**	..	God	..	..	..	.. verse 25
2. **Channel**	..	Gospel	..	..	..	,, 25
3. **Fruit**	..	Obedience	..	..	..	,, 26
4. **Result**	..	Praise ..	..	..	..	,, 27

II. MYSTERY

1. **Age**	..	Since world began
2. **Custodian**		Heart of God. His secret
3. **Disclosure**		By God to Paul to be make known to all
4. **Medium**	..	Paul's Writings
5. **Purpose**	..	Establishment (1. 11)
6. **Nation**	..	Ephesians 3. 1-11

A Fitting Close. We instinctively feel how fitting it is for this most comprehensive Epistle to be closed by a doxology. Its deep teaching leads one to adore the One who conceived so wondrous a Gospel and bestowed man with such intellect to write it in so admirable a manner.

Doxology or Benediction. It is not usual for Paul to end an Epistle with a doxology. He usually ends with a benediction. Romans is the exception.

The Two Endings. Many devout scholars believe that in the two endings to the Epistle to the Romans we have a proof that Paul first wrote the letter down to chapter 16. 23, and subsequently, perhaps during one of his sojourns at Rome, turned it into a circular letter, omitting for this purpose the last two chapters, with their personal matters, and adding this doxology in the rich manner of the Epistle to the Ephesians. As a matter of fact, a very ancient copy of Romans ends with chapter 14, and has this doxology as a completion of it.

The Church Age. Dispensationally, this is important. That is, if we recognise that this is the Church and not the Pentecostal Age. In the view of some the Pentecostal Age ended at Acts 28. 28, when the Jews finally, and for the third time rejected the Gospel. As Romans was written during the Pentecostal Age, before the Church Age with its " Mystery " teaching, there should be no reference to the " Mystery." But the " two endings " explanation explains its presence in verses 25, 26.

The " Mystery." This is the first hint of the " Mystery." To the Roman Christians he does not develop it. That he does later in Ephesians and Colossians.